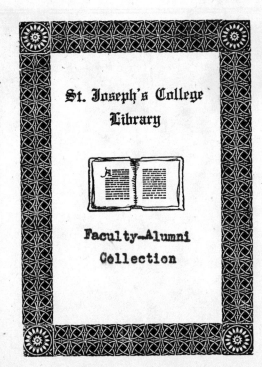

REALIZATION
A PHILOSOPHY OF POETRY

REALIZATION

A PHILOSOPHY OF POETRY

By

HUGH McCARRON, S.J.

NEW YORK

SHEED & WARD

1938

CONSIDERATIONS

PAGE

I

WHETHER THIS BOOK SHOULD NOT BE RESTRICTED TO THE DEVELOPMENT OF ITS OWN THESIS

THE PREHISTORY OF LANGUAGE, A PREJUDICE

ABOUT the use of words by humankind we do not know much more than that, as far back as we can count, man has used them, not as mere signs to indicate his needs, but glorying in them ; through them taking new possession of the things and truth about him. As far back as there is record, he has rolled words upon the tongue, through them tasting the freshness of the real. We must discard, then, all prejudiced theories as to the origin of language, erase from our imaginations the picture of early man, shaggy in bearskin with his club in hand and rattling brains behind a low forehead. For this picture will not be supported by the study of winged words. Many centuries of years before Beowulf came the cry into the air about the poet's city, " I cannot place the post of the winds ; one wave rolls from this quarter, another from that, and we are carried in the midst with our black ship," and Sappho's "ἕσπερε πάντα φέρων, Evening bringing all things home." And by the rivers of Babylon rose the wailing note :

> " And they that carried us away, said :
> Sing ye to us a hymn of the songs of Sion.
>   How shall we sing the song of the Lord
> in a strange land ? "

This is far removed from the baby's indication of want :
" moon, gimme."

TO OMIT HISTORY OF CRITICISM

Just as the writer did not settle down to write any theory, until the facts, as he saw them, had forced a certain view upon him, so he asks the reader not to approach the book with any predetermined view as to what it must contain. We will make a compact. Do you forget that some think letters a literary, elegant fabric resembling fancy stitchwork ; forget too that Hudson Maxim in a fine book worked it all out in the same spirit that had built his brother's machine gun ; that in the opposite extreme the Abbé Bremond in a splendid book has placed poetry just next to the intuitions of unitive prayer. You do this and I for one will not load your minds with all the spiderwebbed lumber that lies in the yard of the pedants. You will not read here, if I can help it, a digest of pre-Raphælitism, the Imagist's creed, Symbolism, or even of Hephæstion's handbook of metre. I do not want to fatten a slim book, which is meant to submit certain positive statements, with rebuttal or precedent. I would not advance with flag aloft in the heroic vanguard of revolution against positions swept and empty. Let us pay honour to the dead in some other form than by recounting their errors and let us state what we think rather than distinguish supposed merits and defects in worthier work. Let us suppose for a moment we could fill in the interstices of this little book with critical precedent ; why, if we repeat all the opinions that have ever been given, we'll never, in such a welter, be able to determine what we think ourselves.

USE OF QUOTATIONS

Let us remind ourselves the study of poetry is not the

study of some one language. There have been those who thought Homer and Shakespeare furnished the best teaching of English poetry. Having recourse most frequently to English poets, I have been bold enough to quote poetry in other languages, usually offering the original, not only for the courtesy obviously demanded of submitting to the reader opportunity for immediate verification, but also in order to offer the real poetry in question.

PHILOSOPHY OF LIFE ENTERS

One further caution : if the art of words is a mirror of life, no explanation of literature can be satisfying which does not include one's philosophy of life. So some of our later considerations will seem to be a word for things rather than a word about words. However, our view of life will be stated only so far as is needed to show that it goes with the viewpoint of all these notes, namely, that wonder need not be sought in any subjective phantasy nor in an unreal fantastic but is to be found in the plainness of the facts.

READER'S ASSISTANCE REQUIRED

So I will appeal throughout to the reader's experience rather than attempt to submit proof. Many of the statements in this book are issued in categorical form for the sake of brevity and are offered rather as questions. I would ask the reader to examine and consider if they are approved by what he has seen of books and of things.

II

HOW A DEFINITION OF POETRY CAN BE APPROACHED AND WHETHER A DEFINITION BE NECESSARY

OBSERVATION AN APPROACH TO POETRY

IF I should have again the job of helping students make inchoate poets out of themselves, I would first direct them to achieve a more intimate acquaintance with the things about them, growing things, living things. To read about the cricket in Fabre and visit him in the field, to meet calves and dogs, know the difference between wheat and rye. To learn to appreciate soil, find out where Castor and Pollux are, how small boats go, how hills differ from hills, what it means to have a city, a home.

SOUND AND GESTURE WITH POETRY

The second step would be, and this should start almost simultaneously with step number one, to see how pictured expression is linked in utterance with sound and gesture. I would have the students produce their Shakespeare, in groups, on a stage. A teacher should show the class how the body instinctively moves in harmony with the voice as we recite Lepanto or Stephen Vincent Benét's verses about the Georgia hill-billy's triumph with the violin—but show also that such union of mind, voice and bodily gesture is present in much less obvious examples than that, is natural in any use of language. A traveller, a figure used to the rhythm of his horse, swinging down from the saddle, necessarily says :

4

" Is there anybody there ? " not " I have come to make inquiries, my dear friends." Now a single example of bad sound :

> " Fail—fail !
> In the lexicon of youth, which Fate reserves
> For a bright manhood, there is no such word
> as—fail ! "

This is tawdry rhythm—mouth it and you will agree—but it is tawdry rhythm because the scene with the old cardinal rising from his chair to deliver that line is tinsel ; the axiom itself from " lexicon " to that ringing " fail " is a lie, not a reflection of reality. It shows Bulwer-Lytton's eyes were shut ; he is not looking at youth or lexicon or failure. Whereas the following rhythm is of the moisture of spring :

> " Whan that Aprille with his shoures sote
> The droghte of Marche hath perced to the rote,
> And bathed every veyne in swich licour
> Of which vertu engendred is the flour ;
> . . . Than longen folk to goon on pilgrimages . . . "

the very sound of it helps convey to us that a natural storyteller has begun. This union is borne out by the drama. Try to write a play with words only. Every young dramatist knows the principle of the advice that Aristotle put in his notes that, in constructing the plot and dialogue, one should place the scene with its moving puppets, as far as possible, before one's eyes. And permit another illustration. Incidentally, in all this matter of poetry, analysis is drawn from illustration, not *vice versâ*. " Wenlock Edge is umbered," take it to the end, that last poem of A. E. Housman's, because the relationship of phrase to phrase is as important as that of one bar of music to its sequel, as the flick of a whip to the swish. " And England over advanced the lofty shade. The lofty shade advances . . . To air the ditty and to earth I." There is rhythm that demands the exercise of imagination, voice, gesture, movement, all in one piece, a human utterance, a sound rhythm. There is the flow, as in music, with which poetry is linked in origin and nature. Just one more. Note the union of sound and sense in Ben Jonson's " Queen and huntress chaste and fair " ; follow it through to " Goddess excellently bright " : such union that one would almost be tempted to be extreme as the Father Castel of the " Colour-Clavichord," quoted by Babbitt in " The New Laocoon," and say there was a light green quality to the sound of the words and the interrelation of phrase.

RHYTHM OFTEN PERSONAL

We might pause to notice how personal a thing rhythm may be. One might venture that the author of " Ah ! Ben, Say how or when " could never have written : " Nay, I am done, you get no more of me " ; although Drayton and Herrick were alike as poets in certain qualities and, even if thirty years apart in age, were raised in much the same sort of world. For one thing, both were educated in a world recently divorced from the Sacrifice of the Mass and the Sacraments, which divorce affected the poetry of Shakespeare.

CHRONOLOGICAL ORDER IN THE APPROACH

After these two steps introductory to the things about us and to rhythm, the student would be fitted to approach books. Here boldly I would adopt the chronological order, not rigidly but would keep it in mind, from Homer to Stephen Spender.

INFLUENCE OF EARLY READING

Of course, some introductory reading from essays on

literature helps the student to discover what men interested in books have found in them. But the reading that best prepares a boy for literature is that done at the age of ten, not in school, but with feet on divan or elbows on floor. He should have read fairy stories or the " St. Nicholas' " or something of the sort. Why? Because it engenders the right attitude. Such a boy has the key. He knows what to look for in books, the dream story that we feel we have read in some book, but which really we have never read ; it is the whole library read and unread together. We unconsciously piece together the ideal of literature from all our reading, one quality from this great book, one or more from that other. Such a student as I have mentioned reads for enjoyment, which is essential because literature is made for enjoyment, not for tabulation.

READING WITH PLEASURE

We should be glad the library is still full of books we have not read. Then we will avoid that stupid worship of titles, that desire to have read for the sake of the name. When reading literature let us read across the page, not down it. Read, careless of ever reading more. True, we should read books over our heads, sharpen our tastes bit by bit. And nothing can change more rapidly than taste. But the soul of this study, if it be a study at all, is enjoyment.

Even the thumbing of a dictionary necessary to the first reading of classics in a foreign tongue must be done, not in the spirit of the classroom, so many lines read, so many more to go, but with the heart centred on reading the story.

NEED OF DEFINITION

Now, this book is not to be on the teaching of poetry

or the kinds of poetry or the history of poetry. It is an attempt to arrive at a definition of poetry. From the nature of poetry are derived the canons of criticism, of appreciation and depreciation. And one's opinion as to what constitutes poetry does make a difference in that person's reading and understanding of poetry. For a poem is read or heard, not only by the eye or ear, but by the mind. Therefore it is useful to approximate, if we can do no more, a true definition of poetry. Many say we neither can define poetry nor need to, and that therefore we should not try. But cannot we try to find out a little more definitely what the thing is? Are we not mistaking the nature of the humble human effort we call definition and mixing it with comprehension? If such an enigma as is man can be defined, cannot literature? And is not this misty attitude toward poetry partly responsible for the study of poetry becoming a study of philology or of rhetoric, of all sorts of things save itself? Is it not responsible again for the neglect of melody which is of the heart of poetry, and for the neglect of imaginative memory? Has this attitude not permitted, and that with high praise, plays without entertainment, where straw figures deliver essays?

III

IF EVERY MAN IS A POET

CAN THE READER TELL?

CAN we determine what poetry is? Can we, the readers of poetry, penetrate the mystery at all? We can, provided we repeat in our reading of a poem what the poet has first done for us. Now in order to consider whether we do in reading what the poet does in writing, let us regard a poem not as a static thing, completed and on the shelf, but as an exercise.

POEMS ARE WRITTEN AND READ

Lest we be worried throughout these pages as to whether by poetry we mean some object or other, as is meant in the phrase about a sunset or an omelet : " That is a perfect poem," or certain notions in the poet's head, or print on a sheet of paper, let me say I mean the poem as being either written or read. If you are a philosopher, poetry formally consists in the final expression of some relation or other between the object or truth and the mind. And truth in imaginative work means not a proposition but things in relation and in action. Fundamentally poetry is the thing awaiting vision. All this we will consider later. Practically, a poem is nothing but black marks on white paper, unless it is being written or read, so we can consider poetry as an act, an exercise of realization on the part of reader or writer.

A POEM MUST HAVE A READER

By exercise in realization, suffice it here to say, is not

meant identification of a poem with the object it describes, but the imitative nature of poetry is implied in the phrase. The poem in itself is something. To say merely what is obvious, it is a series of sounds demanding human ear, imagination, and mind. But the whole being of a poem is imitative both in the meaning attached to the stream of words and in the sound effect of that stream, whether that sound imitate the sound of things as in the words " hiss," " rattle," or suggest the impression made upon the poet by brevity, harshness, change, etc. For a poem to have its formal effect, the author, if no one else, must read it.

THE COMPLETE COMPASS OF A POEM

Poetry is then an attempt to establish some relation between ourselves and some object. The object of the poem can be determined only from the complete poem. " Upon Westminster Bridge " did not have just London for its object, but whatever was present in Wordsworth's consciousness after years of experience. Even so simple a Lyric as " Uber Allen Gipfeln " is not a poem of pastoral peace alone, but of multitudinous experiences of life and death that have coalesced in association in the creator's mind. Often the poet's own desire is the main constituent in this complicated object.

THE READER SLIGHTLY CHANGES THE POEM

Does not the reader repeat in his own poor fashion what the poet did ? Every reader is an inchoate poet. Poetry would have no audience if he were not. And everyone, who has learned words and things, can write a line or two of poetry. Oh ! but the poet is master of a secret. Well what about that selfish pump, the heart of man, does it not surprise you ? Every man in a sense, is his own poet. This reader of ours even changes the poem a bit. To two boys with different childhood associations, Frost's "After Apple Picking," Emily Dickinson's "Train," may bear a minor fringe of different connotations. Everyone knows how a hill where tragedy has taken place assumes in our minds its more sombre shade, how a curve of skyline seems to lose its freedom and become a stodgier, dumpier thing if we have been imprisoned by convention and circumstance nearby.

THE READER REPEATS THE POET'S ACTIVITY

Writer and reader engage in similar activities. Both are passive, receive an impression, the one immediately from the object, the other with the help of the author's reproduction. Both are active, the one cutting his way through an unpathed wood, the reader following in his footsteps. Neither in initiating impulse nor in sustained creative power is the reader so original or so tenacious as the writer, but he does recreate under the writer's guidance. We may regard, then, the two processes as one in a discussion of the relation of the thing to the mind. Just as seeing man receives, acts, reproduces, so writer and reader go to meet, suffer, receive and entertain, focus upon, clutch and secure the term of vision.

IV

WHETHER POETRY CAN STAND FOR LITERATURE

POETRY THE EARLIEST LITERATURE

OF our literature that is still extant, poetry came first. Naturally, with this possession, a certain amount of poetry, in its fist, the race considered whether subsequent writings had in degree the same qualities this poetry had. The poetry was in melody that could be chanted or sung. Some of these later writings were not and yet seemed like poetry in some way. Thus there was need, and has been in the few dozen short centuries since, for some word such as " literature."

Needless to say, we use " literature " as " belles lettres," not in the broader sense expressed in the command to the filing-clerk " bring me the literature of the subject."

COMPLETE COMPREHENSION NOT NECESSARY

Poetry is a loose term but not so as to defy definite assignment. In this passage we should avoid two common faults; either forcing the meaning of the word, contrary to Horace's dictum about the sovereignty of usage, " usus quem penes . . . ," or denying for it, as is often done, any susceptibility of definition. True, if poetry be a reflection, not of ideas or propositions as such, but of real things, then, just as any real thing is incapable of comprehension because related to all other things, so poetry will be subject to the same incomprehension. But one need not know with entire intimacy in order to define.

ENTHUSIASM LEADS TO REPRESENTATION

The trouble with the word poetry is rooted in what has happened in literature. Let us try to reconstruct briefly what has taken place. In the remote past, let us say, something great occurred; the death of a hero; the birth of a god; the growth of a tree. There naturally arose appreciative enthusiasm. Nay, more arose than mere appreciation on the part of the great spectator, man. There was the desire to devour, possess, and incorporate within himself, this splendid thing. Human enjoyment is enthusiasm manifested and fostered in reproduction, reflection (as of the stars in the water), recreation of the reality enjoyed. Such portrayal did historically take place in verse.

HAS OTHER LITERATURE IMITATED POETRY?

I think that such later works, histories, exhortations, panegyrics, novels and the like, as have been held to belong to a special class of writing called literature, have been so esteemed because they imitated the quality of certain earlier pieces that were poetry and had been done in verse. Metre alone had not given the earlier pieces that appeal which we associate with poetry. They possessed what we often refer to as the magic of poetry. Many agree that this magic consists in the reproduction or recapture in meaningful sound of beauty. Beauty seems to lie in the real things around us in as much as they stir a certain affection within us. That affection I think is founded and based on mutual relationship. But of this interrelation, later.

HISTORICAL USAGE OF THE WORD POETRY

To what sort of productions has the word " poetry " been applied in historical usage ? " Poetry," a making, is, as we all know, a Greek word, and the earlier Greek creations or stories we possess were in verse. Although Aristotle says he had no word for literature, the word poetry, a fabrication, a fiction, up to his day seems to have covered the field for the popular mind. That these tales were based on plots the people believed in would not prevent them from being stories. Every good story is, I suppose, if tracked to its ultimate sources, a true story. Fiction, stories, they constituted literature and in verse form. In other countries too were not the earliest stories in verse ?

NATURALNESS OF VERSE

Indeed, upon examination, we find the more regular rhythms of verse go naturally with enhanced and exuberant moods and that what we call prose literature uses in part verse rhythm with admittedly a recurring break, this last to assure us it is of everyday sober stuff, not of the holiday. This companionship of repetitive pattern and exuberant emotion appears, of course, in dance and song too. Possessive and enthusiastic portrayal, not of an abstraction, an idea or proposition as such, but of the real, in a form imitative practically in every way in which language can imitate, and naturally of more constant and apparent rhythm, this was in its earlier days what we call poetry. And this is still the essential quality in those writings to which such words as " poetry " or " literature " have been applied. Poetry is literature complete or perfect in essential qualities. Other literature is so called because it possesses this quality of human imitation, even though curtailed of the natural concomitant of strict form, *e.g.*, verse.

I had almost erased the *exempli gratia* in the previous paragraph because metre appears so often where one does not, at first, expect to find it. It is, of course, in the early alliterative verses and in much that passes as prose or free verse. There seems to be general agreement that Hebrew poetry, not only in the Psalms, but in the sapiential books and Prophets does possess some form and laws of metre.

METRE AND RHYTHM

From the snatches of iambic movement prevalent in our conversation and from the greater regularity discernible in the more emotional passages of a speech or in the more artistic parts of a novel, students have concluded that regularity is the mark distinguishing metre from other rhythm.

FREE VERSE

Free Verse seems to strengthen a belief that verse and prose rhythms are of the same nature. The line of Free Verse, what is it but the phrase of rhythmic prose ? The " cadence " of Vers Libre, the " organic rhythm of the speaking voice with its necessity for breathing," " the lines to flow as they will when read aloud by an intelligent reader," what is it but the phrase of rhythmic prose ? The human voice must pause for breath. An intelligent reader puts the perceptible pause where there is such pause in the sense as we sometimes mark with a comma. The untrained voice naturally falls in pitch at the pause ; is not this the mystery of phrasal cadence ? The resemblance I have mentioned between the free verse and the phrase in rhythmic prose, abundantly illustrated by John Livingston Lowes in " Convention and Revolt in Poetry," in no way derogates from the value of Vers Libre. But, one might object, if the free line is the equivalent of the phrase in rhythmic prose why does not H.D. write :

> I saw the first pear as it fell.
> The honey-seeking, golden-banded,
> The yellow swarm,
> Was not more fleet than I,
> (Spare us from loveliness !)
> And I fell prostrate,
> Crying,
> " You have flayed us with your blossoms ;
>   Spare us the beauty of fruit-trees ! "

instead of :

> " I saw the first pear
>   As it fell.
> The honey-seeking, golden-banded,
> The yellow swarm,
> Was not more fleet than I,
> (Spare us from loveliness !)
> And I fell prostrate,
> Crying,
> ' You have flayed us with your blossoms ;
>   Spare us the beauty
>   Of fruit trees ! ' "

Is not the answer obvious ? In phrasing is there not room for interpretation ? To emphasize the image may she not make the phrase a poet's phrase as it were, provided the harmony of phrase to phrase is preserved, that relativity which makes the extended poem a unity ?

TIME AND RHYTHM

Not to push a point, rhythm anywhere seems meant to indicate organic oneness in an activity extended in time ; and therefore time, equal time intervals, seem to lie at the base of rhythm. Our stress verse in English, where stress is prominent, represents, psychologically, quantity, time. We set it to music, and all verse was originally meant to be read, to have the value of pitch added to its quantity, to be made either a varying chant as in classic epic and drama or a lyric song. Not only time, but to speak crudely, equal time blocks, in which the variety will find play, seem essential for rhythm.

PROSE RHYTHM

I would even say that in such a paragraph as this (from Newman's " Idea of a University ") :

> " If then the power of speech is a gift as great
> as any that can be named, if the origin of
> language is by many philosophers even considered
> to be nothing short of divine, if by means
> of words the secrets of the heart are brought
> to light, pain of soul is relieved, hidden
> grief is carried off, sympathy conveyed,
> counsel imparted, experience recorded, and
> wisdom perpetuated, if by great authors
> the many are drawn up into unity, national
> character is fixed, a people speaks, the past
> and the future, the East and the West are
> brought into communication with each other,
> if such men are, in a word, the spokesmen and
> prophets of the human family, it will not
> answer to make light of Literature or to
> neglect its study ; rather we may be sure that,
> in proportion as we master it in whatever
> language, and imbibe its spirit, we shall
> ourselves become in our own measure the
> ministers of like benefits to others, be they
> many or few, be they in the obscurer or the
> more distinguished walks of life, who are
> united to us by social ties, and are within
> the sphere of our personal influence."

the phrases marked by commas, read by an intelligent reader with the organic necessity for breathing, are equal, psychologically, in the time alloted each one.

RELATIVITY IN RHYTHM

In such a paragraph of prose there is that relation of phrase to phrase that makes the paragraph a unit. This is effected through varying and interrelated quantity, emphasis, pitch and quality of sound. I think the variation within the succeeding phrases of a paragraph of noble prose forms a pattern somewhat similar to the pattern of a Pindaric stanza. (And as difficult to analyze.) There will be repetition of intricate design and culmination. Not that the author of melodious phrasing attends deliberately to such details any more than a great musician thinks explicitly of every individual note and bar. But at some time in his career he must have learned mastery of the details of musical sound. The musician never attained such mastery entirely through playing by ear.

LITERATURE

The simple condition where metrical poetry existed alone, as described in a previous paragraph, if it ever held true in time, did not continue. Even by Aristotle's day, there was a history, Thucydides', that deserved some such title as ours of " literature " but was not in the strict repetitive pattern of verse. In our own corpus of letters there are novels, essays, sermons, all literature.

ORATORY

I am not trying to identify oratory entirely with poetry. But in the essential quality of literature the speech imitates the poem. In so far as it is called literature, it is not a mere presentation of ideas, of propositions, it is imaginative. It is a reproduction of real beauty and, as such, a work handsome in artistry, of course, in itself. It pictures life, is imitative. Not an abstract on ambition, but a brawny Scot, a muscular, murderous poet rushing to ruin, told of with affection for the brute, is what makes us call " Macbeth " literature, and that picturing is the quality in great speeches, in Chrysostom, " You are my fathers . . . ," in Fox, " We are only pausing," in Lincoln, " Four score and seven years ago," that causes us to think of them as literature. Read Demosthenes' third Olynthiac through, and you will see it is teaching and literature both, as are the parables, and literature because it is a picture done with affection for the moving world, at least for that little angle of the earth that smiled for Demosthenes.

THE NOVEL

The novel is a hybrid. It adopted the form of the anecdote as well as of the epic. Thus we have broken prose deliberately following hard on rhythm. For random instance in " Heart of Desire *Darkness* ," by Conrad :

> " A continuous shower of small flies streamed upon the
> lamp, upon the cloth, upon our hands and faces.
> Suddenly the manager's boy put his insolent black
> head in the doorway, and said in a tone of scathing
> contempt—' Mistah Kurtz—he dead '."

The novel often does this to assure an air of realism, that is, to make the reader feel : Oh ! this is true, matter of fact, . . . not in the exalted mood of celebration. Another instance picked for its brevity from Hardy's " Jude the Obscure." After

> " ' Well, I must go, . . . Dear, dear this is awkward ',"
> we come upon : " ' She may swear that on her knees
> to the holy cross upon her necklace till she's
> hoarse, but it won't be true ' said Arabella.
> ' She's never found peace since she left his arms,
> and never will again until she's as he is now '."

It is utterance of the first sort in this example, in such

broken phrase, without sweep or gesture or vitality, that makes the anecdotal, chronicle style. I won't resist one more specimen of such intermingling, from " Tristram Shandy ":

> " ' I am half-distracted, Captain Shandy ', said Mrs. Wadman, holding up her cambric handkerchief to her left eye as she approached the door of my Uncle Toby's sentry-box. ' A mote, or sand, or something—I know not what—has got into this eye of mine ; do look into it—it is not in the white.'
>
> In saying which, Mrs. Wadman edged herself close in beside my Uncle Toby, and squeezing herself down upon the corner of his bench, she gave him the opportunity of doing it without rising up. ' Do look into it ', said she.
>
> Honest soul ! thou didst look into it with as much innocence of heart as ever a child looked into a raree-show box ; and 'twere as much a sin to have hurt thee."

Let us not confuse, by any means, realism, the attempt to imitate the obvious surfaces of reality, with realization, when we meet the latter word a bit later. Realization will gaze upon the same surface which the eye of realism sees. But in realization it is the imaginative mind that gazes, seeing how wonderful it is for the thing it looks upon to be, to be what it is. Do not misunderstand me, I do not mean to depreciate the novel. The novel, if it is not to-day and to-morrow, has been yesterday at least, the medium of expression.

THE ESSAY

The essay ? I would almost say there is no such thing. What common trait have essays save a negative one that they are not finished ? In Montaigne we find a bit of sermonizing, some autobiography, an indolence that prevents the thing from becoming a treatise. Essays are rather notes in preparation than literature. Now the essay has become the light essay containing a dash of story, a dash of parable, a hint of advice. Cicero's, Pliny's, Seneca's letters and essays are, alike, jottings half in form awaiting the unity and finality that make a work.

OTHER LITERATURE IMITATES POETRY

The word " poetry " or its equivalent, has been used with fair constancy to denote what we call literature, this perfect or complete in natural qualities. One boast of poetry's admirers would seem true. Poetry is not only the most intense form of literature, it is " litterae perfectae." The rest is called literature exactly in so far as it approximates, contains, the quality of poetry.

POETRY THE BETTER WORD

Poetry is a more fortunate word than literature in that it does not exclude the idea of sound which is of the very nature of language. Reading literature we still imagine the sound. If we are to have any fun out of literature, let us remember the sound. Why did all the world for centuries memorize poems ? Lucky they if want of print forced them to it. Indeed language is for the tongue. Literature adds a note, the extra idea of permanent, and therefore, written record.

PRACTICAL CONCLUSION

Whatever the truth historically be, and I rather think that people in various times have used both words, " poetry " and " literature " in such various senses that not very much can be proved from etymology, I am using " literature " and " poetry," indiscriminately, as synonomous, save for this following notion. When the narrator allows himself to become fully enthusiastic he will say only the essential, concentrated thing. Or better, he will give only the artistic thing, the imitation of the real without abstract explanation. He will become the seer, and so emotionally seek a more regular and lawful rhythm, be it in novel or admitted verse printed as such.

V

WHETHER POETRY IS AN EXERCISE IN REALIZATION

THE MYSTERY OF OBSERVATION

LET us begin with one of the lowliest of the things that grow. I look, say, at grasses. This I can do even when the grass is no longer visible to the eye. It appears somewhere within me. This is a mystery but a fact to be accepted. Something more happens. The human mind is in awe at this wonderful creation, the grass. There is some sense of interest or delight. Let us take, instead of the grass outside the window, a human action. Some Hamlet stalks athwart my vision. With a greater sense now of intimacy, of completion, the process is repeated. We remake the object of our vision real, as it were, within us and that with some feeling of interest, of union.

IMAGINATION AND OBSERVATION

The first step was done by imaginative memory, was it not? What do we mean by imagination? Let us not attempt a scientific, psychological investigation but accept a meaning in common use. The imagination is accepted by many as the power interiorly to envisage things whether they be at the moment present or not. Imagination rests then on observation. Invention is more a discovery than a creation. For even in the literary creation of a fancied object we cannot make anything utterly new. From what we have seen, we

23

imagine new combinations such as the heroic figure. The imagination is not primarily a power of flying into realms of airy phantasy but the power of viewing real things, in the way in which they really exist, alive and whole, in the round, as it were. It is clear that we humans have no privilege here on earth of viewing, in the way described, that, which is entirely spiritual. Therefore we make no claim for poetry that it is above all earthly power. It is mysterious, as is human life itself.

THE POET SEES MORE

Imagination rests on observation as we have just said, but, when we speak of the imagination of the poet, we mean something more, do we not? We mean contemplation, such quiet viewing of things as we have described together with dawning realization of their significance.

SELECTION OF THE WORD " REALIZATION "

I am going to use constantly the word " realize " because it contains the pith of my meaning. Vision, is too presumptuous, intuition perhaps too vague. Imagination is a slippery word, for, sometimes used in the same meaning as realization, it is used in other more restricted meanings too.

ITS MEANING

The ordinary usage of the verb " to realize " (exclusive of the later financial use of the word), or of the noun " realization," contains a note independent of the presence of the object. In the poverty of language, " to realize " is to make, as it were, real. It implies, therefore, that the real is not, at least not necessarily, present in external intercourse.

REALIZATION A POSSESSION

" Ah, now I realize . . . " while it does not demand present, external vision, would yet say something of more internal pregnancy than necessarily comes in experience from mere dealing with the object. Take any moving object, anything in action, a man raging, or even a man raising his arm, a rabbit leaping, what a wonderful thing it plainly is ! What a marvel that it should be at all ! Its very existence, further its being this and not something unimaginably different, amazes. There is in realization something more of possession on the part of my personality than bodily awareness can give. It is a sort of digestion, absorption, or better, an union, not merely, however, on the part of the imagination.

QUIET STRENGTH OF REALIZATION

There is the object itself, there is thought about it, midway, as it were, there is realization. One given to the practice of mental prayer would know it from the process of contemplation as distinguished from both consideration and meditation strictly so called. Authors speak of this realization as quiet, as leisure and yet intense act, as in the depths of our being. It grows as a tree with the rain pouring on it. There is strength and comfort in it. There is joy in it as there will be in heaven. By what power in man does this realization take place ? The whole man, soul and body, seems to realize.

THE WHOLE MAN REALIZES

Realization is on the part of the whole man, therefore, of the vivifying human spirit. It is of the human mind, which term, I think, should include both imagination and intellect whenever we speak of human, mental vision of the real as we know it. Realization is a comprehension on the part of the intelligence and imaging power working together. The act of realization cannot be located in some one faculty. Some Scholastic treatises seem anxious to conceive any operation as proceeding from some one power or other in man's make-up. Such analysis would not be helpful here in treating of realization. Living actions and experiences are those of a unit. Throwing is not so properly of the arm, nor even of the body, as of the man. Sight is not, as such, the performance of the eye, but of the man. To see is so needful for life. When the imagination sees, it is the living man who sees. When the mind sees anything, it is not rightly the faculty or power, but the living organism that perceives. Man can use several powers together in one action. I think you would more than agree that poetry is not necessarily first thought of in pure intellection, then imaged in phantasy, and later done in words. I have an important reason for prefacing here that, in any human action, it is not some power of the man, but the man who acts. In general, that reason is, that it is a man with his whole make-up at the time who writes poetry, not a single faculty.

REALIZATION A HUMAN ACT

Where realization differs from imagination in the narrower sense is in that, while we attribute imagination to the cow, we would not use of her the human term " realize." We would not say the cow in the stall realizes how good or how beautiful the grass is. She can see the grass. In her dreams she imagines herself chewing the cud. Never does she realize the meaning of the grass. Ah ! here we have it, realization is a grasp of meaning, of significance. We see something, a flying bird a hundredth time, and wonder at such a being dawns on us. We can only express it : " Why should such a thing as this living, flying thing be ? To exist at all, how amazing ! " This meaning consists for any limited not absolute being in relation. What that relation is shall be the purpose of this book later to uncover.

REALIZATION OF TRUTH

Throughout this essay I will speak of the realization of things. Hence the verbal difficulty might occur that in ordinary speech we never speak of realizing a thing, but rather a fact. For instance, we say : " now I realize what it means to be in love," " now I realize what loneliness it," not " now I realize the tree." In response let us consider, is not the ultimate fact always a thing ? The fact that the tree is green is really the tree as green ; the important reality is God loving us rather than the fact that God loves us ; the truth that two and two are four is found in potatoes, tomatoes, hats, and all things. The reason that most of our important truths are in proposition, rather than in the simple apprehension of an individual thing, is because our limited things never stand alone, they are in relationship always ; they indicate and in combination constitute the facts.

REALIZATION AFFECTIONATE

To realize differs from imagination in that it is an act of the whole man calling into play feeling as well as intellectual, imaginative sight. The imagination sees ; realization sees in a sense of union with the object, with awe, wonder, and a certain affection or joy. Joy ? Many a time when we use the phrase " now I realize " in this life, it is of sorrow we speak or disillusion. Perhaps not even noble sorrow ; we have eaten of the tree of life and the taste is flat. Even in this realization there is that sense of possession, of union with the experience, with men in sorrow, with life.

REALIZATION NOT IDENTICAL WITH ACTIVITY

To consider certain other properties of realization. We stare long at a beautiful blue lake and the first rapture will not return. We pass by something a hundred times and the hundred and first we see it. We must make a certain effort at honesty and freedom to penetrate, and yet truth comes as if from without. There is some cause from without of realization. We may strive and sweat after an illusive thought. The work helps, but the vision of the truth comes, as it were, somewhat casually. Note in this connection that a certain rest and centreing of the soul is a desired condition before the essential thought can strike. When we are too Martha-like in sedulous attention, our own activity prevents reception. This effect takes place perhaps in all concentration, where a centreing of attention implies some degree of relaxation. Although receptive, realization takes place within and is active, not entirely passive. We must distinguish realization from experience ; it is rather the possession within myself of that experience ; it is not the experience itself. How many a tramp has seen all there is to be seen and hardly had a thought. Within we make that dramatic reconstruction which enables us to say : " Oh now I see, it is real to me. Previously I knew, I had been told, I realize now."

A SUMMATION

Poetry makes us realize. To realize seems to include to view as real, that is, to consider the truth submitted as it occurs full-bodied in the moving real things around us. The imagination, then, has its part in realization. To realize seems to include the note of contemplating, gazing, rather than reasoning about. To realize seems to be a sympathetic appropriation made with a certain affection.

REALIZATION AND POETIC INTENSITY AND CONCENTRATION

Realization is the secret of poetic intensity and concentration. The poet has tact, the touch and feel of things. When the poet sees in a flash the thing as it is, he does not have to expand explanation about it. " Long-shadowing spear " (accept it for the moment as correct translation), gives us the sunlight on the sand, the figures separated and menacing, the dread of darkness coming over a fighter's eyes. And, as the poet becomes more and more immersed in his story, intensity mounts climactically from one high note to others of a piercing quality unsuspected hitherto by the reader.

REALIZATION AND ORIGINALITY

From this realization, this " making a truth one's own," comes that sincerity and originality pertaining to authorship. Such originality contains sincerity as its essential note. It is not necessarily the originality of something never before seen on land or in the sea. On the contrary, poetry's creation is a humble imitation. But there is an originality that indicates that the truth was digested and absorbed by the author. The impression received has become interwoven with other impressions in his head ; there has been appropriation, possession, so that it comes forth now from the integrity of his personality ; it has been his own, nay more, a part of his mental activity, of him. We would say then, at the end of this passage, that, in all plainness and earthly sobriety, the poet sees things with love.

c 2

SUPERFICIALITY

The superficial comes from the want of this test by imagination, from not having made the thought one's own, from not having absorbed, realized it. If one wants an example of superficiality that will not be cavilled at, let anyone, who has, against his will perhaps, a store of axioms dinning in his ears and a stocked vocabulary, make the following simple experiment. Shutting off the mind as far as possible from the contact of actual experience, breaking the circuit between imagination and reality, start a speech on education. The flow of words in a sort of free wheeling will surprise you. It is the poet in us who is sane, an unbeliever in words without things, and a kindly satirist. The poet's imagination insists on trying to view what really is, rebels at the often-mouthed sayings that roll and reverberate so hollowly. Though we must admit that great ones among the poets have certainly loved the roll and thunder, the sound and music of words, yet the sounds were their own.

VI

IF THE REALIZATION OF POETRY MEANS TO SEE WITH JOY THE REAL

TERMS INDICATE THAT THE POET SEES

THE first movement in writing or reading poetry is to see, with feeling, if you wish, but to see. There is common agreement that it takes a seer to write poetry. All the terms in use imply substantial concord in this, such terms as vision, intuition, imagination, realization, imitation. The classical juxtaposition of prophet, seer, and poet would imply the same.

SIGHT COMES FIRST

Now the first step in all this is to see the external object. Homer was not born blind. Incidentally when speaking of bodily sight, we will use the sight of the eye as the most important of the senses in a meaning inclusive of other sense perception. To see the outer object is the beginning. Perception of colour and form and movement is only a beginning, but let us not hurry away too fast, for much has been decided if we agree that this is the approach. Poetry is then more contemplative than meditative. It produces that, which, with apologies to all who have written against confusion in the arts, we call a picture.

BEAUTY HAS BODY

" To-morrow and to-morrow and to-morrow . . . " there is the picture of poetry beginning to form. Not, mark you, the monotony of time but the tedious march of time. It is not done with a brush. Where is this parade—down corridors? If you wish. Note how the sound, the appeal to the ear and voice, contribute to the " picture." "And all our yesterdays have lighted fools . . . " note this picture goes to other times and other places. The common opinion that imagination is at the bottom of all literary production would seem to mean that all agree the writer and reader must see something. The very idea of a personal viewpoint and an embodied or " in concreto " object of imitation would bear this out. The corporeity (or, if you have the sight of a pure spirit, at least the individuality) of the beautiful would satisfy this idea of a " picture." Beauty connotes some real and individual thing. For instance, take the definition of the beautiful as St. Thomas words it : " quae visa placent." We take pleasure in the sight, not of an abstracted quality, but of things real and substantial. It is enough if we are agreed that the universal abstraction does not stalk, paler than any ghost, an idea and no thing, across the pages of literature. The pigment and line of painting need not be present. Indeed, reading a book, we do not see a complete picture, with the flowers all in place, of the bank Oberon knew, nor all the staircases in order in the house where the murder was done. Neither do we enjoy such simultaneous vision when we visit a real house, a real bank. But if one examines :

> " How hard is the way up a stranger's stairs."
> " That I may not be a burden on the ploughed land."
> " Under the shadow of thy wings, O Lord."
> " In the beginning was the Word and the Word was with God."

there is the scene, the moving picture. The picture of poetry is not a photograph. The root reason why it is not is that, while it is the expression of experience, it is of experience that has been incorporated in the whole body of the author's thought, that has been made his own, possessed. But there is, whether in clear colour and lines or left indefinite, the scene, as it were, albeit a moving scene as we shall discuss later. Poetry's outside object then and its own work is embodied, individual. If Poetry begins with sight, its power lies, not in spider-like projection of thought or emotion, but in active relationship of give and take between eye of body or mind and the object of their gaze. If not only the critic and reader would realize this, but if the creative artist would let the object talk to him, as it were, might not the subsequent processes go more surely all aright, if reader and writer would not break away too soon from this, the start?

VIVID SENSE PERCEPTION PART OF ARTIST'S EQUIPMENT

The definiteness of opinion, of like and dislike, which a teacher notices in a young creative writer as distinguished from other students, springs from the vividness of his sense of form and colour, from the fact that he uses his eye, exercises a power of vision, consequently exercises his imagination too. For imagination depends on sense knowledge. It cannot make from nothing.

APPRECIATION STARTS WITH SIGHT

This very sight of what lies around us, of itself, contains the demand for further insight from a poet, a man. The cow for all the violet in her eyes has not exhausted the possibilities of vision. Still the first step for a class in poetry is an appreciation of mud and grass, not to mention beetles and weasels. It will lead to contemplation.

A YOUNG POET BEGINS WITH SIGHT, RATHER THAN WITH MENTAL THEORY

A young poet starts by really seeing things to which the rest of us, until he speaks, are blind. But then his friends perhaps gather round him, or some dæmons from the current whistling atmosphere. There is discussion, he wants power, and lo ! he has a theory, or parts of several, on life and art, and his work is too soon " sicklied o'er with the pale cast of thought." It would seem then that the enemy of good workmanship, of good making, is the enemy of human nature—pride. If we would only let objects speak to us instead of greeting them, as they advance, with : " Oh ! yes, you fit into this or that pigeon-hole I have constructed for just such an object, such an event." St. Paul made the same complaint that men would not really see with open mind the world around them, " so that they are inexcusable." Poor humans, we, who cannot make even a picture of a really new animal, who cannot make a tree, but have the divine right of utterance, why will we not express the obvious ? There is such wonder in it.

A YOUNG POET'S PROCESSES, CONTINUED

Let us attempt to approximate what the young poet in his best moment really did. Come to the low window. Out there the grass. He looked at it and let it come to him. Why this and not something else ? Why shaped like a dividing knife ? Why green ? And then, what at [*why*] all ? The questions are meant to indicate, not so much deliberation, nor even immediate rumination, as the poetic awe. If they have value as an indication, then it is things he sees, and the realness of things, more vividly than other men. That which we call poetic wonder is then initially a solid, substantial attitude. It might be said that the poet's gift or talent was a more cogent sense of reality than the rest of us, caught and webbed in blinding superficial activity, are permitted to possess. He, who doesn't love language—definite, advancing words and their power of portrayal—doesn't love life enough. Part of the joy of living is in the expression of vital interest.

POETRY CONCERNED WITH THINGS

The texture of poetry is of actual things. Look at Keats. The best of him is where the drawing of things is clearest. Merely the word for the thing is there, with a phrase or an adjective to point it, to dimension it for us, or perhaps the simple noun ;

" of candied apple, quince, and plum, and gourd."

there it is, the real joy in what he sees. Perhaps in Homer, more than in any other, one can find it. It is clear in his use of epithet, in the enthusiastic unwearying counting of fighters, clans and swift, black, well-made ships, in the naming of town after town, the seaside one, the rich-in-flocks. He delights in things, he loves them, he sees Hecuba's robe :

" ἀστὴρ δ' ὣς ἀνέλαμπεν· ἔκειτο δὲ νείατος ἄλλων,

it shone as a star : it lay below the others."

It is not an illusion the poet suffers ; it is the only too rare privilege of using his eyes. It was not a queer metaphor Andrew Marvell was trying when he tells us of oranges against the shady leaves :

" Like golden lamps in a green night."

He suffered sight for an instant, and saw the solidity, the greenness, the thickness, the actual leaves present there.

POETRY CONCERNED WITH THINGS, CONTINUED

Sappho's last red apple, and Coleridge's last red leaf, are triumphant memoranda of human beings using their eyes. Keats' stained glass and candy and wine and key and casements are the same, and Chaucer's tendre croppes and smale foules no less than the holy blisful martir. Something of the wonder and rareness that is in all created he catches in the clerk's twenty bokes, in the wife of Bath's ten pound head-kerchief, in her hosen of fyn scarlet reed, in the Shipman's beard, and more than all, in the pilgrims themselves, nut-head Yeoman and courteous Prioresse. The poet will see, realize, " drink deep, deep," and then poetry is forthcoming ; a simple cry :

> " O brave new world,
> That has such people in it ! "

even such naked words :

> " O Erd', O sonne,"

or

> " Tantum ergo Sacramentum . . . "

POETRY CONCERNED WITH THINGS, CONTINUED

What some of us naturally remember most clearly from Vergil are not so much the gnomic utterances of stern-minded endurance or the like of that universal line that tells of the world's tears, as rather the cave of the winds and the bees, the storms, Priam's mangled body on the shore, Dido peering into the whitening dawn, the pilot up at night, on the beach, watching the stars, ships sailing through the friendly silence of the quiet moon. But I must admit most of us love in any author the rolling sound, the elocutionary roar of many a line where the stage is deserted save for the soliloquy, sometimes

deserted, alas, even by meaning. So we know Polonius'
advice is all very fine, but surely more solid, realer, are
those places where a " willow grows aslant a brook,"
and where Oberon and Titania met :

> . . . On hill, in dale, forest, or mead,
> By pavèd fountain, or by rushy brook,
> Or in the beachèd margent of the sea,
> To dance our ringlets to the whistling wind, . . .

THE GREAT LINES

The objection is advanced that the " great lines "
often have nothing of the picture, of colour, line, definite
shape. Besides the answer that all speech is symbol and
the entire stuff of words a fabric of metaphor, look at
the most abstract of these, and see how it is bright,
meaningful and rich only in its links with a picture. There
is a last line in a Greek play :

> " στερρὰ γὰρ ἀνάγκη, hard is necessity,"

that is, without the play, an inert truism, but come upon
it at the end of a story, brutal with the frenzy of a ruined,
enslaved queen, loud with the cries of a Thracian mur-
derer, his eyes torn out, and ending with frightful
prophecy, the short words are as sad as earth and deep
as the heart of man. Again, what is there here, in the
poem that is itself the perfect picture of the nineteenth
century :

> " Ah, love let us be true
> To one another ! "

except when we hear it by night, at the window, listening
in the sweet air to the grating, melancholy, long with-
drawing roar of Dover Beach ? The idea is there, not a
bodiless abstraction, but, as it is in creation, a real thing.
Poetry is a word for things.

DIFFERENCES BETWEEN PICTURE IN POETRY
AND PAINTING

In the line from Keats' " Of candied apple, quince and plum and gourd," the change in the manuscript from " sweets " or " fruits " to " apple " may show how much broader is the use of " picture " in literature than in painting. In literature the portrayal always includes the suggestion offered by the sound and flow of words, as well as by their associative value in the reader's mind. Poetry is a sound picture. Just as previously we used the eye for all the senses, so we must bear in mind that a poem in its portrayal of reality appeals to the auditory imagination as well as to the visualizing. All poetry is onomatopœic. Take any lines :

> " I know a bank whereon the wild thyme blows,
> Where oxlips and the nodding violet grows
> Quite over-canopied with luscious woodbine,
> With sweet musk-roses and with eglantine."

Note how the change from " o " to shrill " i," the recurring mutes and the " w " and " l " help in the representation of the wealthy and bright aspect of this bank. It would not be fair to stay with " A Midsummer Night's Dream," with such lines as " creep into acorn cups and hide them there " or phrasing such as " Are we all met ? Pat. Pat." Not only in such lyric dramas but everywhere poetry uses sound.

ONOMATOPŒIA, ASSONANCE—FURTHER THOUGHTS
ABOUT THEM

A number of text-books and essays have demonstrated that alliteration, assonance is constant in literature. Let us mark a few of the alliterative affects in the following lines.

The sestet of one of Gerard Manley Hopkins' sonnets :

> " O the *m*ind, *m*ind has *m*ountains ; cli*ff*s of *f*all
> *F*rightful, sh*ee*r, no-*m*an-*f*athomed.   Hold them ch*ea*p
> May who ne'er hung there.   Nor does long our small
> Durance d*ea*l with that st*ee*p or d*ee*p.   Here ! cr*ee*p,
> Wretch, under a comfort serves in a whirlwind : all
> Life death does end and each day dies with sleep."

Note incidentally the labour and hesitation, with which one must read the " o " and the initial " m's " of the first line of the sestet.

The lines from " The Merchant of Venice " :

> " How sw*ee*t the moonlight sl*ee*ps upon this bank.
> H*e*re will we sit and let the sounds of music
> Cr*ee*p in our *ea*rs ; soft stillness and the night
> Become the touches of sw*ee*t harmony."

From Shelley's song of Asia in " Prometheus Unbound " :

> " My soul is *an* ench*an*ted boat
> Which, like a sleeping sw*an*, doth float
> Upon the silver waves of thy sweet singing."

I cannot avoid giving some space to the importance of sound in poetry. Onomatopœia, as well as alliteration, is not occasional, but everywhere. Not only does such a line as : " Like snow on wool thy fallings are " ; force us to read softly, but every passage of good poetry tends to lead the reader to a suitable vocal interpretation. The quality of the various vowel and consonant sounds helps in portrayal as well as the other qualities of sound, namely, time and the varying pitch, more delicate in difference in the spoken word than in the regular intervals of a musical instrument, and the shifting stress of emphasis that gives a centre to word or foot or phrase, to the smaller and larger units of rhythm.

OF WHAT THINGS DOES POETRY TREAT?

Poetry is a word for things, but must the things poetry portrays be taken from external nature? Why so much talk of earth and air, rock and water in poetry when we live in apartments and subways? Why not more, for instance, of New York. Well, what is New York? A rock—such rock for builders—set in the midst of water, through which a ship of any draft can make its way. What are subways? Man-made tunnels to pour humanity through. Wonderful, but even more strange is that delicate tin toy, containing so many adjustments, the fires in it starting so many times a second, running, not across a parlour floor, but scurrying all over a countryside. However, it is earth and rock and water, on which we move, from which we make all our clothes, houses and vehicles, wherefrom we feed. We breathe this air that blows around the globe.

WHAT NEED OF POETRY?

In a discussion of this point, that poetry portrays things, the question arose, is not reality more beautiful than the imitation? Was not Dan Plato right in regarding the imitation, poetry, as weaker than nature's reflection of the ideal or divine original? Is the poem " Nod " more beautiful than evening? If not, why not discard it, keep just the evening herself? Sun, sheep, honeysuckle, shepherd, are more beautiful than the poem. Ah ! but the poem, says someone, makes vocal that evening. There is the mind of man at play in this reflection. Catullus' bed can be an " imitation of an imitation," but the poet's creation has been given more utterance than the carpenter's. Sunrise is a reflection in the sky of a divine vitality, if you will ; Browning's " o'er night's brim " is such a reflection in an answering

mind and heart. You might prefer to put the answer:
" The poem is a beautiful piece of work in itself," " a
voice in itself." But the subsumption would come—
" the poem's whole being is to imitate. It is beautiful
only as an imitation." So you would be saying, finally,
the same thing as the first answer. The poem is utterly
an imitation, true, but in human accents. The object
has been transmuted by its gestation in the breast of man
into a vocal thing that can render formal glory to God.
It is human enthusiasm expressing itself in imitation.
Granted that the mind does not work until startled by
its view of the thing, yet poetic experience possesses the
thing, the thing as significant, as a creation, a sign, one
of the lesser words of God, a very obvious message and
positive, telling how good the complete reality must be,
the fulness of the longed for.

THE BEAUTIFUL IS THE REAL

If reality be then the poet's engrossing object, beauty,
that *splendor veri*, will not consist in some aura or halo
superadded to the naked truth. Beauty will be formal
reality with only one added note of visibility to complete
its comprehension. The realness of things, the individual
reality as such, subject to vision, that is beauty. The
capacity for pleasing the beholder is in the very concept
of perfection, of existent being. So all things should
please had we eyes to see.

UGLINESS A PRIVATION

To the Scholastics ugliness is, like evil, not an absolute
entity, but a misfit, an ill relation. Scars are of beautiful
crimson, wrinkles could be lined up in a harmony of
beauty; they seem inconvenient running across some
human faces. But the detailed answer to the question of
ugliness, nay the answer to change and progress, to

limitation and being, to the one real question, I will attempt to indicate later. Ugliness is abundant, plain, and stark. Evil is everywhere, and not grand but drab and monotonous. But we should not shut our eyes to the plain fact that creation is a marvel, the obvious object full of wonder, the plainest action a source of awe and reverence. Wonder in it there is :

> " Wet falls, a lilt within the light of days.
>   Something goes singing down the leaves' thin veins.
>   This night, the motherly dark like rich loam, prays
>   Upon us black and clothing blessings, rains
>   Over us the holy drops that join in fair
>   Comfort the good pig with the upper air,"

not to make mention of little beasts, machines, and men.

WHAT IS THE EFFECT OF POETRY ON THE READER ?

If beauty be the object of vision, the æsthetic reaction will be a joyous contemplation. The " finis operis " of poetry will not be to stir the waters of any of those human emotions that impel to action. It will be rather such activity as is a satisfying term of effort, a blessing, not a summons. The first immediate and natural effect of reading the Iliad will not be the surge within the reader of the wrath of Achilles, but a perception, a reproduction, a possession of as much of the Iliad as he may grasp. This perception is a joyous possession. Always that, it varies in different acts of course. A contemplation of a rose is as different from the contemplation of the Iliad as the rose is from the Iliad, simply because such perception is reproductive.

WHAT IS THE POET'S EMOTION ?

" Reproductive," and why am I a sensitized plate for all creation that comes within my ken ? Why have I this appetite for what is without? There is in some unknown form an union amongst all us things. We want more of reality, more life. This is our work, this is our play. Call the feeling the poet entertains for the real, joy or love or affection or sympathy or a sense of union; that is the emotion in which the poet and his reader see.

VII

IF POETRY IS INDEED TO SEE RATHER THAN TO FEEL VARIOUS EMOTIONS

POETRY IS SAD

POETRY is very tragic.

> " The anguish of the world is on my tongue.
>   My bowl is filled to the brim with it ; there is
>   more than I can eat."

—from Edna St. Vincent Millay—or Hamlet's lines :

> " I loved Ophelia : forty thousand brothers
>   Could not, with all their quantity of love,
>   Make up my sum.   What wilt thou do for her ? "

This is forthright expression of emotion.   Quieter but perhaps equally intense is the dead phrase of Macbeth :

> " . . . She should have died hereafter.
>   There would have been a time for such a word."

So too from Shylock :

> " I pray you give me leave to go from hence :
>   I am not well . . . "

Equally quiet and more philosophical, yet not without intensity, is :

> " And so, from hour to hour we ripe and ripe,
>   And then from hour to hour we rot and rot."

Poetry is such a distressful creature.   Almost as sad as we are.

44

POETRY FILLED WITH EMOTIONS

If the immediate effect of literature upon the reader is perception and not directed to the emotions, why and how is literature so emotional? To answer: first, real sight must be affectionate. This affection is the poetical emotion of writer and reader. But perhaps you refer to the various emotions of pity, fear, rage, loyalty, such as prompt men to action, and this I have said does not satisfy your difficulty. After reading Ruskin, Winchester, Connell—shall we include Aristotle's famous sentence on the Katharsis—you want to say to me: " But poems do rouse me to pity. When I read Achilles' words, I do feel wrath at Agamemnon. All the lines of poetry are full of the various emotions." Well, that is true. Life is emotional. Perception is reproductive. A tree or the Iliad is necessarily anthropomorphologically received. Why so? Because man is our life and therefore our language. The Imagists objected to the cosmic poet as out of place in a universe no longer Ptolemaic. But in a certain sense it is inevitable that our talk betray man as the centre of all for us. Just as we cannot imagine any universe of a different kind, for what would we picture, other stars or other creatures of this same matter, these elements, with space and motion and time? We are bound by its terminology; so our terminology is defined, nay born, from our sense experience in race, in country, in locality, in family. But above all in humanity. It is a human life we lead. Our language then will define all things in terms of humanity. If our life is human, is man, our language must be human, in terms of man, and his life will form our language. Human emotion then is thread after thread in any tapestry, piece after piece in any mosaic we gaze upon. If we receive and build a reproduction within us of these emotions, and if that rebuilding is done in the sympathy necessary to all cognition of the existent, we too may readily smile or cry at play or story in the moment after, but first we will see.

MAN IN POETRY

The function of the various urgent emotions in poetry may be clearer if we consider the presence of man in poetry. As Aristotle rightly assumed, our object, and therefore our language or expression, is the picture of man. Put a man in your block of marble, a man on your stage. The actions and the words of man compose our language, for he has the lime and the dust in him, the cabbage and the rabbit, and what else do we see? He gives the formal glory, for he too has the words, and what other words do we know? And what is this fellow, man, always about? Feeling, is he not? Raging or sorry, loving or hating, yelling or in joyous peace. Then, in your picture will appear these threads. But the æsthetic perception of this tapestry . . . that is a pleasant, an enjoyable, a joyous contemplation or beholding. In the immediate æsthetic act, which is intellectual and imaginative, there is, since all knowledge is reproductive, a picture of these emotions. Having that reproduction, that picture in my soul, I might readily, in a subsequent act, proceed to have a similar emotion myself—this subsequent act is not the æsthetic.

EMOTION THROUGH THE PICTURE

If the poet should desire to communicate to us his own indignation or fear or hope, he must do this through his work. His work pictures to us that which aroused the emotion in him. Even the music of poetry is imitative. The natural and immediate effect then of his work will be to offer us sight of something.

THE POET MUST CARE

Mere recording of a disparate object or event will not suffice for poetry. The poet sees with affection and manifests intense personal interest. Granted the loneliness and lost quality as it were of beauty, expressed by James Stephens in the lines :

> " Under a lonely sky a lonely tree
> Is beautiful. All that is loneliness
> Is beautiful ",

yet that loneliness must be discovered and discovered by one who cares. The poet feels a relationship within him to the object and is aware of the relationship of that object to many other things. It is the object as thus related that forms the complete vision before the eye of the poet's mind. Sight leads the poet to associate, combine and to possess. It is worth considering, as we will in a later chapter, whether things are interrelated in fact. This I must say in advance, that I think the emotion peculiar to the poet is based on a marked sense of the relationship of other things to himself and of things among themselves. Rhythm itself seems to arise in some sense of comradeship with the things around us.

THE EMOTION AROUSED IS ONE

The feeling then, aroused by poetry, of the very force of its nature as literature, is specifically one. It is that joy that invests the act of contemplation. The individual act of perception, being a picture, will of course only adequately be described by the presentation of as much of its object—book or plain or tree—as is absorbed by the reader. That is why it is so difficult to fulfil the order : " describe the emotion or thought of this poem." Because the poem images with possessive feeling, that is, it realizes. To name adequately the real object is a very large order, seeing it is coloured and joined by manifold association with my other experience. To name satisfactorily in other words than those of the poem the complex emotion portrayed or rather suggested in the pictures of a poem will never seem possible.

PASSION MYSTERIOUS

Human passion, true as good, and false as hell, lasting as the throbbing of life, passing as wind-blown ash, a yearning of the body yet the whole world of spirit away from that, verily it belongs on this earth where the bird flies, and the bird is torn and tortured, where all things seek union and reach out for pain, where some child has played with the tempests of will and desire.

EMOTION PORTRAYED INDIRECTLY

The passion of man, we need not study it, we will only make fools of ourselves. For, not any saint nor sinner, but the Maker alone, can make any sense of us. The artist and the student should pay attention to the picture, the moving object. Feelings will take care of themselves.

IMAGINATION THE SOURCE OF POWER

The picture is the source of power in literature more so than the direct emotional appeal. Since for the reader, the appropriation, the realization, the " now I see," the making of a truth one's own, must come in his own reception, in his own mind, why, then, the power which recognizes that fact and does not try to force, the imagination that simply submits its portrayal, will have more effect emotionally.

THE TEST OF EMOTIONAL REACTION

But when we read a poem or story, do we not test it by the emotional reaction within us? To determine if it be literature or not, is not our practical test: does it grip the heart or cause a catch in the throat? Yes, but must not something catch the emotions of the writer before his book about it will so affect the reader? Is it not the thing described, the object of the awakened vision that really grips the heart? And when the power of vision is awake, is not any reality capable, if really seen, of evoking such emotion?—If seen with a dim awareness of what it really means?

PAIN IN THIS REACTION

The joy of contemplation is, we must admit, a human joy steeped in a certain tragic sadness. It is true that the sight of beauty, particularly moral beauty, creates in us an emotion close to tears. As Pan Michael's moustaches bristle for the last time it is as if we saw something lonely and lost. That pain affects all our art is not surprising, since it affects our life. I think we should reserve thought of it to a future chapter.

VIII

IF POETRY SEES AN OBJECT OR IS A SUBJECTIVE AFFAIR

IS FORM PURELY SUBJECTIVE?

Do we create beauty by our appetites? Is the beautiful nothing but the pleasure we fond mortals take in the sight of that, which, left to itself, is formless chaos?

IS POETRY SUBJECTIVE?

Am I admitting that beauty is subjective? If I did I would be contradicting the truth that seems to me too obvious for demonstration, that lies at the basis of the whole paper, that things plainly are wonderful in that they exist at all, in that they are such and such, shaped, coloured and moving. I cannot believe all perception an illusion of the race. If it be not an illusion, then perception is the right word. Something is apprehended. That something is real. The real can give delight to him who possesses it by title of cognition; the beautiful is the real. Beauty in act is, of course, the real as related to an observer. Poetry is personal in that a man's whole body of thought at any stage, his whole intellectual experience as a unit, influences his expression, gives peculiar meaning to his words. As poetry is not a statement of precision and abstraction, but an intuition of reality, a realization or grasp of the object as it is actually, poetry rising in such a perception, expresses the object as assimilated, incorporated in my personal whole at the given moment. In this sense poetry can be called subjective. It expresses the thing possessed. Look once more at Keats' " Ode to Autumn." There is possession by the poet.

IS THERE ANYTHING PURELY SUBJECTIVE ?

There is no such thing as the purely subjective. I would have no experience if there were nothing to know. There is reality, objective truth of which my own feelings may be a part when I describe them. There is association within the mind. If this association be unfounded, if there is no such relationship in nature, there is falsehood and bad art. Thus youth is an experience, fear and sickness are too. If, in old age, copying maxims without testing by recurrence in imagination to what I've seen, which test is an exercise of realization, I should say my youth knew no fear of sickness or of death, then this is false.

CONTEMPLATION SECURES A POSSESSION

I have not stressed any difference between contemplation, a process of vision, and possession, a physical acquisition. It would run this way. The boy seizes the apple and eats it. That is the joy of possession. He admires its round red curve on the bough. That is joyous contemplation. But a scholar objects, " Is not the taste one of the senses as well as the sight, and does not your contemplation belong to all the senses ? " Well, I have neglected the distinction between possession and contemplation because to me at the present time this seems true, that the most complete physical possession (we are not speaking of juridical relations) we can have of a distinct thing (remaining such, *i.e.*, distinct) is by contemplation. In digestion the apple ceases to be an apple. In contemplation, while there is union, there remains separate identity.

POETIC CONTEMPLATION IS ACTIVE

The impression received is not utterly passive reception. The waves of light strike the eye, but it is the man, the artist, who sees, and to see he must act. The impression the artist receives is also an active possession on his part. Now, if to contemplate is to possess and to reproduce within myself, we can understand how literature can be both an objective impression and a personal expression.

Come see, here is an object, a tree. Now here is the poet's mind, Kilmer's, that knows already of Our Lady and the Church and the Jongleur and the mediæval cap and bells and plain khaki. The tree enters that mind and out come the romantic and yet plain lines, joyous and humble: " Poems are made by fools like me, but only God can make a tree."

RECONCILIATION OF THE PERSONAL WITH THE OBJECTIVE

If literature depends on a perception, which is possessive, then it is a personal expression. The thing is seen, it is by vision reproduced within me, that is, it is possessed. It enters as food of the mind, therefore is incorporated. It sends out tentacles, as it were, within my mind to all the other knowledge there, it establishes relationships with the whole body of my knowledge at the time. In fact, this body of knowledge is like the busy electrical activity of a dynamo rather than still. " Tentacles " was an inadequate word because, by this relationship within my mind, the new or latest possession is modified, assumes new characters in relationship. This activity of mine is my personality at the time. When I express, then, what I have seen, the vision as expressed will come out coloured by my whole personality. You understand I am not contradicting a permanent personality, but a person does grow and does change accidentally. Indeed, a person can regard even himself as a thing apart, an object. The object, the tree of Kilmer's poem will be expressed as in relation to the other objects he was thinking of. If this relation were entirely of his making it would be false. But happily in his poem it is founded in fact. Even outside Kilmer's mind the tree really humbles a man and exalts its God.

IS POETRY A WEAKNESS?

The subjective critique of poetry seems to me largely responsible for the notion, so often repeated, that artistry in words is to be attributed to some fault in the construction of the artist's personality. But this would lead us too far afield.

IX

IF THE MIND CAN SEE AND IF POETRY
BE AN AFFAIR OF THE MIND

TRUTH THE MORAL LAW OF POETRY

I THINK that we might discover that deep down the reason why we do not thoroughly enjoy a given poem is because it is partially false. When we say that Cowper, at times, in his narrow self-preoccupation lacks universal appeal, do we not mean that, considering the message of his poem in its implied view of life, we find we cannot entirely agree with him? While we are enjoying the devastating quality of Swift's sardonic bitterness the taste becomes cloyed. I rather think it is because we feel that, along with much truth, there is untruth there. Truth and nothing else, appeals to all, all the time.

POETRY TEACHES

A poet's opinions are a part of his poetry, no matter how often it be denied. Shelley is a teacher in every line, his teaching, nihilistic, so simple as to be confused, had nevertheless truth in it. The aspiration after something never seen on land or sea, after perfect liberty, is in the make-up of every man. When Shelley thought that perfect thing was to be found by naive trust in nature he erred. In the belief, expressed in his poems, in the existence of sweet souls constituting the natural elect, I think he erred again because I believe each of us can be mean ; all are ignoble. But Shelley wrote great poetry because he expressed the need of enthusiasm, a great truth. Again, A. E. Housman's idea that all ends with the grave is true to the eye of sense. After the last book is written and read, there will still be a question in the heart of the last man that only death can answer. We Christians believe there will be an answer.

THE POET REFLECTS HIS AGE

I selected A. E. Housman because I think he is the representative of that state of mind we would call transitional between the nineteenth and twentieth centuries. Poets seem to give us the attitude of mind of the body of the people in their age more truly than many books. But every age has a share in the work of the poets, because people have had the same thoughts in Athens and feudal castles. We all have our share in the poet's imaginative philosophy, if it contains a deposit of truth. A poet's philosophy does mesh in the fabric of his poetry. What is utterly false cannot be beautiful, because it cannot be real.

ART SELECTIVE OF NECESSITY

Art must select. The novelist, be he ever so laborious, could never give all his character's thoughts even of an hour. Macbeth's breakfast talk, his readings, and what connections his life had with the affairs of some peasant down in England, are pieces in a plot too dark and complicated for any human head.

THE IDEAL

Once the artist offers an impression, a universal truth, an idea in embodied form, not only the individual Macbeth but something in the character of interest to all of us, then, freed from the trammels of a too comprehensive enumeration of buttons and trivial activity, he will look for the heroic, the ten-foot figure, he will portray " better men than of our sort," the man who is true to the intensity of nature stripped of ordinary inhibition. And heroism or greatness, in so far as it is real and not illusory, can be naught else but some sort of goodness.

SENTIMENTALITY *versus* REALISM

However, this idealism of great art can degenerate into a sticky falsehood in the sentimental stories, a falsehood that represents life as a baby-pink and blue nursery for the sweet-souled. Then some realist will rebel. In this realism the world and life can be represented as altogether trivial, when to open eyes there is evidently something great and marvellous about it all. Most insidious of all for the multitude, sometimes the art of words has descended to the misrepresentation of life as comfortable, average, calling not for heroism, but for the ordinary, that misrepresentation which contradicts the experience of every living soul and yet has misdirected more lives than the devil with its false assurance that mediocrity and lukewarmness will suffice.

POETRY AND OBSCURITY

I suppose that every bit of poetry demands, in greater or less degree, penetration. We readers should be willing to re-read. Metaphysical poetry is not deliberate obscurity, it is rather a tribute to the intellect. But I do not think that this justifies the cult of obscurity. Speech, the instrument of the mind, can convey thought, can portray real things and universal truth in earthly metaphor, but there is much that it cannot do. I salute the sentence that does not attempt to carry every nuance or connotation, the brave sentence awaiting assent or denial.

THE TERMS "IMAGINATION" AND "INTELLIGENCE"

I hope no reader will be offended by my use of the terms, imagination and intelligence. Imagination, in its narrower sense, will stand for the ability to reproduce in material and extended mental image, even when the external image is no longer present to the senses, such features of a sense perception as have impressed, and to form a new image, not absolutely new, but built from previous reproductions. Imagination in the broader sense, in which it is often used in text-books about poetry, will include the immaterial intelligence. We cannot emphasize too often that intellect and imagination co-operate in the poetic act. This act belongs specifically to man as man, neither angel nor beast. Permit one example to show how a clear perception of poetry as the product of co-operating imagination and intellect may help to clarify criticism. How are we to judge the "Poetry of Wit," either that of the "Metaphysical Poets" or that of the "Pseudo-Classical Age"? The former, when they were not engaged in the rapier play of pun or euphuism, used all natural and homely objects as signs, emphatically as signs, of something deeper appealing to the mind. The latter often reasoned in verse, more often indulged in epigram. When idea and picture are simultaneously present in the work of either class, we unhesitatingly call the work poetry; if both are not present, we are perplexed and are forced to elaborate defence.

INTELLECT AND IMAGINATION CO-OPERATING IN POETRY

Permit a brief review of the way in which intellect and imagination work together in poetry. A poem is the outer expression of the contemplative awareness, of the contemplative apprehension. "Contemplation" is used to indicate the gaze that takes in *things*. In seeing things, mind and imagination work together in a fuller way than they do when the mind is deliberately abstracting and the imagination can furnish merely a concomitant symbol, a dot, for instance, for simplicity. The scientific treatise, as such, abstracts from the object a quality and discards the rest. Literature, although it too is an activity of the human minds and offers ideas, yet continues to view the thing in the round, as an individual and therefore complete separate thing. A poet, engaged with the greenness covering nature, would be imaging, at least vaguely, the spread of green waters, fields and forests. A poet, impressed with numbers, would still see the numerous stars, buildings and men. When we examine the various theories concerning the nature of literature, an assumption of this imaginative quality seems to be the starting-point of all. Therefore I think we may regard such imitation of reality as the first distinguishing mark of literature.

THE UNIVERSAL

The world of thought is practically a world of universals. We know what is common to many. But the universal, for instance, " human nature " is not found in formal loneliness in poetry ; we find there a character so acting as a man that we of the audience feel we could stand in his boots. Or, again, we find in a poem not fatherliness alone ; we see Odysseus acting as a father. The universal exists in things, for example, being is in everything. The universal exists more properly in the Ideal Being, Who is Being in the realest sense of the word, Who, if we could say it without irreverence, has all the virtues and values of Plato's perfect bed, rest and repose in the fullest, that is the most perfect sense.

INTERRELATIONSHIP OF THINGS AND TRUTH IN POETRY

Things in this world seem to have common roots. This we will discuss later. But these common roots are the foundation of what the text-books call the universal in poetry. This relationship of things is also the foundation of metaphor. And poetry is the expression of the universal in metaphor. If the metaphor you express in a poem is true in nature, your poem is true ; if the metaphor is founded on some obscure relation in fact, your poem is true. Poetry is " more universal than history," because, with human mind, not merely with mechanical eye, poetry sees the common note, the kinship existing in nature.

INTELLIGENCE ESSENTIAL TO POETRY

Any theory of poetry that minimizes intellection minimizes appropriation, the fierce passion of man for cognitive possession in the mind. The abiding passion is not in matter but in the sore spirit. The thirst for truth is not for a mere sentence. This chase of ours must find not thought but what we can ride home with, that we'll wave the brush of, run down, caught.

X

IF THE OBJECT BE IN ACTION AND IF POETRY BE THE TELLING OF A STORY

SIEGFRIED kneels beside the running water, behind him Hagen grips the spear. Charlemagne hears Roland's horn and the conspirators tell him Roland is but hunting. In a suburb a young couple form a new family. In all three cases there is a common note, the note of the story.

MOVEMENT IN POETRY

Poetry is a story. This does not contradict that poetry is a picture. It is a moving picture. It is a sequence of associated images. The picture of the old woman in Kristin Lavransdatter or of the old nun in Sierra's " The Kingdom of God " depends for its strength on the whole previous series of pictures. That magnificent picture of Anna Karenina is only magnificent because of the charm of Anna in the earlier chapters.

Poetry is a moving picture, a story. Why ? Because the things poetry portrays are moving things, and poetry portrays things as they are, moving ; secondly, because human life is a story ; thirdly, because the imagination of its nature is a traveller. What you hear of enshrinement arranged by literature, of the " fixing the eternal moment " need not contradict this. The litera is a somewhat permanent thing itself, but the object, life, is not represented as dead. Literature does not pin life as a moth ; the wings can still flutter in the story.

MOTION IN THINGS

The objects that poetry handles and portrays are moving things. There is nothing static in this world (not even those minds that you suspect of remaining still). Indeed, after reading the mathematical physicist, one almost concludes that if there be an equivalence of mass with energy, if time is motion, space or extension motion, then matter is nothing in its ultimate constitution to our prying eyes save that God wills it to be, which would be enough to make it something most emphatically but a great mystery to us. Things are moving. Man, who lives here, made of earth, is in constant change and motion. Even his knowledge comes primarily, remember, from what he takes in through open eyes and ears. How intimately connected are we with all the change going on about us ! The air we breathe, the oxygen entering our blood, the wheat we grow by, grown in turn from soil, air, rain and sun. More strictly we advert to change in the mind of man when thinking of a story. However, we see that change of soul in changing face and moving body. Furthermore, soul and body constitute one man, changing ever.

MOVEMENT IN HUMAN LIFE

The core of poetry's content, human life, is an emotional tragedy. Prayer, journal experience, and poem concur in this. Life is a risk, a change externalized. And what more do we need for a plot ? The objects then of poetry's portrayal are many stories. These stories seem fragments of a mirror we cannot construct, of one larger tale, the story the creator makes, since all things seem interrelated in action and reaction, in space and time and life. But this last thought we must leave, perhaps, with God.

THE IMAGINATION A TRAVELLER

The faculty that produces poetry is a traveller. The imagination of its very nature goes to other places and other times. In relation, it finds its words and its truth. The " picture " in poetry is not restricted, as is the painting, to one place or time. This also would lead us to think that the art of words gives something like a story.

STORIES AND RECREATION

The story, risk, suspense, change and catastrophe, would seem to be not only the life but the recreation of the race. Witness any ball game, any adventure. The story is mirrored in all our games with their essential element of suspense. Therefore all recreation would seem not only in effect but intrinsically to justify its name if it be vicarious life. It is not then to derogate from the dignity of art to call it recreation in every sense of the term. It is right that our recreation should be in our poor way a re-creation, imitating " the becoming " of nature and life. For the desire for more life, even " vicarious life," is founded ultimately in the root desire of all the finite for more reality, more being, perfection.

THE PLAY A STORY

The drama is a story, and all poetry is dramatic. The division into dramatic, narrative, and lyric, is a good distinction to aid in a teaching of form ; but narrative poetry has the essential material of the dramatic in the struggle of its hero and the dramatic way of telling in its suspense, even though it substitutes : " Now he told him that," " δή," for direct reproduction of conversation. The lyric, the enthusiasm proper, the relish of a truth told or assumed as told rather than the telling, was a part of the drama. The drama springs from the gestures of a narrator, and gestures are also expression used in descriptive narrative. Narrative poetry and lyric are closely connected with the drama.

—NATURALLY SO

Neglecting the historical genesis of the drama, what would we ourselves do, if, off in a village of our own, a great event occurred? We would declare a holiday and celebrate. Our tribute would take the form of a representation. We would live over again that great event. Being enthusiastic we would adopt the more repetitive, unit pattern of dance and song intermingled with recitation and stage activity in our representation. Beauty, that is reality, particularly great and universal reality, the which could be put in other words, " something in action manifesting a universal truth, a truth we all can enjoy," rouses enthusiasm ; enthusiasm leads to imitation ; the imitation will be a story with words and actions ; the words will be partly song, the action dance because of the enthusiasm.

LYRICS HAVE THE TASTE OF A STORY

Poetry was originally a making, a story. The stories were in verse. The song was inchoate dramatization. The lyric is even to-day the relish, so to speak, the enthusiastic retasting that implies a story told or suppressed. Whether the names in the story be true or not, in other words whether history or fiction, is not essential. If it have an intrinsic motion of the soul, a change externalized, it has an action, a struggle, a plot.

Poetry is a story. This picture the imagination offers is in motion. There is portrayed in every complete body of literature, such as can be called an independent unit, an interior change, manifested, exteriorly embodied and shown forth.

DID THE ANCIENT AUDIENCE KNOW THE END OF THE STORY?

There is really more than just suspense in a good story, there is an element of doubt about the outcome. This should be, if the making is a making, and therefore of something new, thus imitating creation and reality. We are too quick to assume the Greek audiences knew the end of the plot. Witness the (1451 B) " Poetics " " Subjects that are known are known only to a few and yet give pleasure to all."

" Τὰ γνώριμα ὀλίγοις γνώριμά ἐστιν ἀλλ᾽ ὅμως εὐφραίνει πάντας."

SUSPENSE AND SURPRISE

Suspense is at least an illusion of coming surprise. Granting that the opening of the mysterious door in the " Arabian Nights " brings disappointment as the hundred and first elephant in a Roman Circus must have done, granting certainly that a new realization of something often seen before is the better gift, let us not despise the marvellous in stories. We have to admit there are strange fish in the ocean and wonders unnoticed, unseen in the doings of the grasshopper in our fields.

SUMMARY

The one, single or dominant impression will be of reality in motion; this reality will be man; the work that gives this impression will be, then, of a change in man's soul, if it be concerned with an idea, a truth; this change, externalized of course, the work of the imagination; there you have a plot, an " action." The plot will be merely inchoate in some bits of literature, implied in others, present, I think, in all.

We must dwell here again on the presence of human emotions within the story, for their presence is inevitable. If we analyze away from the text-books and theories, we find we want to-day what we wanted at ten, a story. We wanted something of a plot then, but the same ten times over, if it gave us a thrill, smiles or tears. Smiles or tears, particularly tears, were not alone desired in themselves as a katharsis, but because they flowed from an enjoyment, a joyous perception of something we thought fine.

Now then, in reading a story there is an identification with the characters consequent upon their presence in my perception—that identification is a vicarious life. Incidentally, then, the admiration of art if it be founded in a desire for life is not a mere admiration of the cleverness of the imitation, such admiration as is expressed in the chill phrase " How like ! "

Poetry would seem then to be a picture of life, of moving and interacting things, and therefore active in its portrayal.

XI

IF THE JOYFUL POETIC CONTEMPLATION BE ROOTED IN THE INTERRELATION OF THINGS

WHY DOES THE POET LOVE THE THINGS HE SEES?

WHY this love of things on the part of the poets; of ocean by all from Homer and Vergil to Byron and Yeats, of earth and farmland by Wordsworth as by mediæval lyrists, of sky, of men by all? We have just determined that poetry must be active to reflect reality. Now, is the activity of moving things founded on mutual relationship? Is the meaning in real things that causes wonder and joy to the poet, is this meaning in some relationship of these things amongst themselves, to the poet?

THEY ARE RELATED TO US AND INTERRELATED AMONGST THEMSELVES

We come now to the core of our content. Why should the poet be interested in the grass? He seems to view it as a gift. Even writers who deplore the sick water colours upon this puddle, life, in their very interest, infuriated if not enthusiastic, would swing the universe at the wrist. The real poet does seem sensitive to beauty; at least he has feeling of kindred, of kinship with things. Amidst all this we see, we are here; we never leave; we are made of the soil, we have the dust and water and lime and chalk, the life of vegetable and animal within our make-up. We breathe this air and feed on imprisoned sunlight in our bread; with every breath we return. This interrelationship is interpreted by the human spirit, which, while it informs most intimately, transcends and can view it all. These binding ties are at the source of poetry, poetry which sees things, realizes things, tells of things with love. These roots of ours in earth, coupled with the kinship of all things, the incomprehensible unity of individual things that still remain themselves, seem to me to constitute in general the object of poetry, in other words to be what poetry treats of.

PHRASING BETRAYS THIS

The writer must enjoy. His vision, meaning what he sees with the sense eye, the imagination, the mind, must be written with enjoyment. The very phrasing, as for instance that gathering and loosing of phrasal energy in the intellectual passion of Shakespeare's sonnets or the furious fencing balance and thrust of a Bellocian paragraph, will betray this enjoyment. Some of this is exuberance in the richness of words, but that very revelling of the artist in the word rises in the discovery that the symbol can help him to play the re-creator. The writer must feel as he sees. There must be, then, a sympathy, a kinship with the thing seen, a relationship. The root of this enjoyment in vision, the sudden eye-embracing possession of other reality, is to be found in the perception of relationship in the thing to ourselves. We feel that we and what we see are part in one bigger thing. This thought again perhaps gives key to the emotional and personal character of literature.

TWO EXAMPLES

What is the difference between two pieces that one of them should be great poetry, the other not? We know the sonnet sequence of Edna St. Vincent Millay, which contains " Loud days that have no meaning and no end," is poetry, and are not so sure that what we have seen of the same poet's sequence, "Conversation at Midnight," is poetry. Why the distinction? We say because the latter wants the emotional appeal or because it lacks the beauty of the earlier work. Yes, but why is this lack? I think because the later sequence treats reality without the enthusiasm real things deserve, without the perception of our relationship.

KNOWLEDGE SUPPOSES INTERRELATION

Indeed in all visibility is there not a universal communication of which the pollenization of blown seeds is but a faint figure? Does not all the reproduction of cognizance demand some sort of identification of the distinct? The sympathy of knowledge would seem to have root in a common blood-stream, so to speak, running through the universe. The mystery of contact between seer and sought seems to lie in a real relationship that could be expressed tentatively; while all things are severally, really distinct, yet they are really united.

THE UNIVERSE SEEMS TO BE ONE

All we have considered would lead us to conclude some sort of connection between things, some sort of union. This, of course, does not mean they form a one with the compactness and intimacy of our personality. The universe seems to be one sign of something, a sign of a paradoxical unity founded on real distinction, and therefore in our human view, on difference and dissension too. I do not wish to build a chimerical theory. In sobriety, the universe as we see it doesn't fit any cute man-made theory. Daily we meet strife, ignoble meanness, the drab monotonous, the impenetrable. Yet there is that wonderful harmony.

IS THIS THE BASIS OF POETRY?

Why hitch all this on to poetry particularly? First, because of that affection required in portrayal of the real, of embodied truth. It implies some awareness of union in things and with things. There can be no true union with, nor affection for, that which is utterly devoid of kinship and common roots, in whose veins runs other liquor. And, whether we like to admit it or not, we have an interest and affection for the rest of creation. Secondly, on account of the very nature of rhythm, particularly the more stringent rhythm, metre. Variety and change in unity and return! We've heard it compared to the slashed breeches Michelangelo designed for the moving legs of the Papal Guard.

THE POET SEES, TO A DEGREE, INTERRELATIONS

The poet, with sight and insight, will see the relations of things. Everything seems to be related in some way to everything else. So that our several human words are to show some part of a more complete view, a view hidden and unclear. Every author seeks to penetrate to some meaning. Does this last mean that the poet has to indulge in world synthesis? Good heavens, no! It means quite the contrary, that his work may well be to tell us of a tree or mountain brook or of himself, God bless him! I meant to indicate not what the individual poet should aim at, but why poetry is concerned with the relationship of things among themselves.

THE INTERRELATION OF THINGS IS IMPLICIT IN POETRY

There is poetry, which directly expresses the union of all things. But I think I would only weaken my point by quoting such poetry. For all poetry, all writing with affection, rests, to my mind, on the interrelation of all the things we know. Is not this the trouble, which perplexes Hamlet : the combat, in ferment, between a feeling of isolation from all the world around him, finally not undesired and amounting to disgust, the combat between this feeling and a sense of immersion, union, and all that union implies, with the rest of creation ? All surrounding circumstance, rather than just Lesbia alone, provoked from Catullus :

> " Odi et amo : quare id faciam, fortasse requiris.
> Nescio, sed fieri sentio et excrucior."

It is the labour in the very marrow of a creature.

THIS RELATIONSHIP AFFECTS THE VERY STYLE

" Daffodils that come before the swallow dares and take the winds of March with beauty." That word " take " suggests the capturing of a fortress, possession after storm with pinnacled flag ; it suggests standing alongside the foe with free hand and free lance, the exulting liberty of slim power not titanic, not cumbersome. How the movement of the verse fits with the word " take," from " come " to " with beauty." Such suggestion, constant in poetry, valid because of some constant relation in reality, shows that poetry is the expression of, and depends upon, a family union amongst things.

THE TWO RELATIONSHIPS CONNECTED

The two relations of things amongst themselves, of things to me, are joined. There is a meaning in this or that to me because there is a meaning in the universe.

RETROSPECT

There is a relation of things to the poet. To absorb a new form we must have that form in some manner within us already. To form a reproduction within us we must have within us the materials to make that reproduction. That realization should be possible, the thing itself must in some way be in us. We must be material to appreciate grass, with vegetable life within us, with something more, a divine spark because the grass has that too. The poet major who has special gifts, the poet minor in various degrees of development in every one of us, sees or perceives externals. It is natural, inevitable, and ordinary, and therefore he should and must, to be a poet, indulge in or exercise this vision of things.

RELATIONSHIP ESSENTIAL TO THINGS

But this is not enough. And why? Because more is calling to us from that very grass we view, from the very green of it, the points on it, the swaying of those points, more than we have yet mentioned. We do not superadd, but rather look more steadfastly at the object under our eyes. Let us see what happens. Here enters a principle. It is not so easy to put in words, is rather a sense of reality, but might be stated thus: that the various qualities of real things *are those things themselves* manifesting certain aspects or bespeaking certain relationships. For example: the beauty of the dawn is nothing extra, distinct from the dawn. To apply this principle here; the object of the poet's sight, the tree or the grass or the child, the form, colour, depth, material and movement, in themselves contain the idea of, or call for in their very being, what the scholastics have called a " ratio sufficiens " of that being. This " ratio sufficiens," this inevitable " why? "—and " why? " is not a superfluous question echoing in empty corridors of inanity; no, " why? " and " what? " are ultimately, as we have just attempted to indicate, the same question—this pressing, insistent " why," what is it in answer but God, Who is everywhere, Who is.

Why or what is the grass ? The reality or truth of any finite being ultimately stands in some relationship.

THE POET SEES THE ESSENTIAL CHARACTER OF RELATIONSHIP

The poet has some faint perception of kinship with all things, and of the fact that all other things are kindred amongst themselves suffering a faint nostalgia. Every artist who works at imitations has a partial perception of this interrelation, and this perception is the foundation of the emotional theory of poetry. The whole mystery of affection, in a universe that is vestige and shadow, mirroring the Triune God, Who is Love, the mystery of hate and ill, cannot exist save in kindred, save in beings that can know, feel and possess each other. The " Welt-schmerz " of the great artist is not merely overwrought nerves. The nerves are keen and tactilely feel and call to his mind some faint pulsation beating, beating through it all.

THIS AWARENESS NOT CONTRARY TO REALISM

None of this excludes realism. Provided he has not developed ophthalmia of the inner eye blinded by the colour of Como or a sewer, the most stern realist, if the other faculties are not dwarfed by over-developed sense habit, can see in the very reality under his eyes all this. It is ordinary reality that gives birth to wonder and concern. On the other hand, the most ardent fancy should still admit that it does not comprehend. The reaching arms of the mind are ever frustrated. The picture is never wholly taken in. We read in Aristotle (1448 B) " Poetics " : " Poetry seems to have sprung from two causes and these pertaining to our nature, from the instinct to imitate . . . and the natural desire for harmony and rhythm." But this desire to imitate reality in harmony and rhythm is founded in the natural tendency to acquire and possess more reality, greater perfection of being. This desire to incorporate is legitimate if things really are related to each other and to the artist.

THIS THE MAIN THOUGHT OF THIS BOOK

In this booklet the chapter I would emphasize is the one we are just concluding, and in the chapter, the thought that the things around us are interrelated in some way amongst themselves, such interrelationship offering the foundation for poetry. For the essay as a whole intends not so much to develop the explanation of the unity in the world offered by the Christian Church as to recall to our attention that visible unity itself, which seems the basis of all affectionate speech, of all poetry. That interrelationship and unity of the distinct things that make up what is visible seems obvious. As a further step I believe that the only explanation lies in the belief in an intelligent Maker, and in the Christian faith. That is why I introduce into this theory of poetry the chapter that follows.

Before proceeding to our next consideration, let us rehearse briefly what we have so far proposed. Poetry is primarily imaginative, an affair of sight and insight. By imagination we mean, in this connection, grasp by the human mind of real things, not in abstraction, but as they exist, somewhat in the round, as it were. These real things are distinct and separate, but interacting as in a story or fragment of a story. Such action upon one another is the evidence of their interrelationship. This interrelationship is the object of poetry.

XII

IF THIS INTERRELATION OF THINGS BE FOUNDED IN THEIR RELATION TO GOD; TO THE WORD OF GOD; TO THE FULNESS OF THAT WORD

IS GOD THE CORE OF THIS INTERRELATION?

UNITY appears more clearly if we consider that vital force informing the whole, the only possible reason of being, or better, The Being of being. That Being of all beings is God. God the Creator, God the Sustainer, the Mover, God, Who is in every breath of wind and blade of grass, in office buildings and subway trains, making every second anew, moving all movement, working as it were, has appeared in the person of His Christ, the Son of God. The secret mystery of reality seems to lie in this relationship at the very core of being. There is something at the root of being not to be explained by the finite mind. Why is the grass? There have been many ways of ignoring the question, only one answer ever vouchsafed. God is in the grass, making, sustaining, living in it. It is the something in existence itself not explainable. May it be the mystery of real relations in God, the substantial love, mirrored in creation? There is the mystery in poetry. The mystery of poetry is the mystery of being. Please note that nowhere am I advocating any semi-material " atmosphere." Such things as grasses and people I can see, and I can believe in the intelligence that made them. " For the invisible things of him from the creation of the world are clearly seen, being understood by things that are made."

If that conceited little story-teller we call the poet is granted the humble wisdom to see God working in the grass, he is faced with a great thing, the total that forms in its various parts and phases the proper object of his vision. All and any of these external objects he beholds standing in this cosmic park are, by internal force of their very being, interrelated and united. This seems true from the unceasing and returning interaction of their external movement. The light is coming now from some furthest star. Some have spoken of the universe as like to a body of water in which, if aught move, all moves. Nor is it mere outward effect alone; there is the constant giving, taking, absorbing, of all forms.

WHERE IS THE INTELLIGENCE ?

When I speak of all we know constituting one larger thing, I do not mean to attribute life and intelligence to the universe, save the life and intelligence of God. The young poet should be sure to read Henri Fabre's " The Mason Bee." The young mother building her nest does the wonderful thing she does, he shows, not with her knowledge, but in the way Socrates attributes to poets, in a lesser sense inspired and enthusiastic.

PANTHEISM IN POETRY

With creative art in mind, one is led to think that there are three steps or grades in opening our eyes to the things around us, and that the first and the third may make poetry while the second does not. They are : love of this or that small thing, bare disillusion, love of the whole of life. The need of this third is what brings so many poets in their maturer work to some form of the protean worship of Pan. In " Rousseau and Romanticism," Irving Babbitt has offered evidence sufficient to show how devout the Romantic poets were to nature.

> " My altars are the mountains and the ocean,
>   Earth, air, stars,—all that springs from the great whole,
>   Who hath possessed, and will receive the soul."

And we can find equal manifestations of various and vague devotion to the congeries, the heap of things, in other periods. Vergil and Goethe, Euripides and Nietzsche, Tennyson and Marx appear to have sought their gods in the flaming soul of the universe, in an evolving omnipresent love, in reason, in Manichean Night and Day, in grooves of progress, in an inhuman humanity. But how can there be hunger for that which is already identical with me ? Real distinction seems essential for union, for enthusiasm. Mythology with a personal spirit for every tree—trunk and spring seems nearer to truth than any form of pantheism. Admission of the individuality or distinction of the separate things in the universe seems to me necessary for any just consideration of the larger whole we speak of. Above all, it seems necessary for the keeping in touch with reality, the view of real things essential to imaginative expression or poetry. There can be no joy, no wonder, no realization, as the poet experiences them, without something distinct from self.

MONISM

A further caution, lest I contribute to a facile monism. I do not mean to deny a very real conflict between good and evil nor to deny the possibility of real evil, that is permanent and lasting will for discord. You see we Christians believe there is a real problem. We believe in sin and hell, that there is evil not just a theatre show of it. The Redemption is from real trouble. We do not think sin is in man, cruelty inherited from the saber-toothed tiger and greed from the jelly-fish, but from human choice. The hurt is due to a fall. We believe truly in change and chance, in possibilities one way or the other. The will can choose.

> " Dame du ciel, regente terrienne,
> Emperiere des infernaux palus,
> Recevez moy, vostre humble chrestienne——"

THE SUBSTANTIAL LOVE

The reason why God made the world is because He is as Dante says : " L'amor che move il sole e l'altre stelle." Love is that which any child knows and which none of us can define because we are too material, self-deceiving. As love is the spirit that moves the Whole, so in descent it is the motive in every action, the tendency to union while preserving the real distinction, without which there can be had no union, only one sameness. Deliver us from the dull porridge of the Monist.

This chapter is not offered as apologetic to prove the existence of one God. The chapter so far has been a brief indication of what one, who believes in God, believes to be the complement and explanation of the preceding. So the subsequent paragraphs on the Word of God and the Christian people are but a suggestion as to how the preceding facts of nature find an explanation, to the mind of one who believes in Christianity, in the divine Word of God.

CHRISTIAN BELIEF IN A PERSON

In what does the Christian believe the beauty of creation to be founded ? What is for him the root and source of enthusiasm ? I will try to indicate what the

F 2

practical answer is, not in theory, but as it exists. Such an answer, rapid as it must be, can be little more than a suggestion of the lines of study, wherein that answer may be discovered. The Christian answer, folly that it may seem, is to be found in an Individual, a Person.

The great distance that still persists in our minds between the Absolute Beauty and a creation containing death and evil is traversed by the Word God has sent us, the God-Man. He, by his death, gave light and life to the world. He is the explanation of the problem of evil.

CHRIST AND EVIL

Motion demands a change. A story demands a change. All reality as we know it postulates a change. In the very notion of matter lurks change. Dissolution of everything in nature precedes or accompanies, follows fast upon, fusion. This in the inanimate. When we come to life the same process continues. The fuller cat depends upon the mouse, the hawk upon the sparrow. Here we can manufacture no answer save what God's story vouchsafes us. Change, pain, ugliness! It is the only problem of life, and in this we must confess we are not gods. What does the story of Redemption, revealing that in creation and in the Creator which was hidden from the foundation of the world, reveal to us? That God in his prescient omniscience saw the descent and death of his divine Son, to redeem a *real* evil, to be a good greater than any pain or sin could be evil. Out of the heart of the evil, then, comes such good as could not elsewhere arise. God seems to have permitted and used evil as the material cause of good. Only God could do this.

When in many a play we see character perfected in trial and infirmity, we are witnessing a partial expression of the great truth that in this world evil is the material of good. Dante was right. Through some realization of hell is the road to heaven. O yes, we should learn κανόνι τοῦ καλοῦ, by the standard of the fair, but it is pain, sickness, or some liability that is converted into gentleness, wisdom, power.

THE MEANING OF LIFE

What is maturity, growth in life, but an exercise of realization, looking back to realize what mean and cruel seeds would have grown within us but for the Cross, looking forward to realize how our dreams must finally fructify in the wood of the Cross? If I made this indefinite and said that suffering is necessary to growth, so much any ripe experience would approve. We Christians believe the meaning of life is centred in the Cross of Christ.

CHRIST, THE CENTRE OF THE UNIVERSE

In the liturgy of the Catholic Church this most intimate of Words is portrayed as the heart and substance of all creation, unto the glory of the Father. It was just for that reason, was it not, that He became a separate individual creature. It is so important to remember this, that He is an individual Man if the realest thing in the world is not to become a theory. He is the pattern of all things. The rock, the sea, the mountain, the sky, human activity, are all to symbolize Him and therefore are they real things, real separate rock, etc. All things were made for Him. He is the term of all things. He is King until he hands creation back to the Father. He is the cut stone that supports the arch of His Church. He is The Sum of Mankind, the Man.

CHRIST, THE KEY TO HUMAN LIFE

He is the Key to the intensity of life. Incorporation into God, or loss of it, alone explains the want of proportion necessarily inherent to any creation by an infinite God. And this want of proportion is the glaring puzzling disharmony that bothers all artists (because it bothers everyone else). For example : we are so small, our desires and our reward or punishment so awfully great, nay long before that, the good or harm we can really do, so great.

CHRIST THE UNION

If Christ then be the heart and core of reality, the hidden mystery of the universe, which poetry would dimly see, we may well pause a moment. I have said above that, even naturally speaking, it would seem to the eyes of man who had not heard the words of revelation, if he looked long enough, that all things were in some unknown sense one. One, while they were separate, distinct, individual entities. The Catholic hears and believes that Christ, the Word of God, is that union.

OUR LORD A DISTINCT PERSON

So, too, it is necessary to bear in mind that He is a distinct, individual Man. All this mystery of the elevation of the insignificant, our incorporation into Christ depends upon the fact that the Second Person of the Most Adorable Trinity became a Man, distinct and individual, Whom we might know and love, became one of us to pay the price upon Calvary, to share that price and what it bought in the Eucharist. That we may become one with Him, members of Christ, it is first essential, I repeat, that Christ be a distinct individual Man.

CHRISTIAN ENTHUSIASM

A man came to earth, Who was enthusiasm incarnate. His virtues or qualities of soul flamed in eagerness all together. The balance in his soul was not produced by quenching any single flame, but because wisdom fired as high as mercy. His patience was not a curb, a duty, but was a fond and foolish eagerness. He had the virtues of a father. We never think of the fatherliness of this Man, yet it is natural to suppose that He would reflect the virtue of the Father Whom He loved above all. Now this Man offered a gift. After each rejection he gave anew in more lavish and extravagant forms. The gift He wanted men to accept was the sonship of God. We must not divorce any instant in this Man's life of giving from any other. Incarnation, Cross, Resurrection ! They are all to give one thing, and his Death is the centre, the payment, the earning. Christ redeemed us from sin. But how positively He did it ! He made us in that redemption children of God. How ? He said, as it were, to his Father : " Lo, they are one with Me, Thy only-begotten Son." This, not by nature ; there'd be no gift then, and yet not by any legal fiction, but by a real quality given to our nature—a right to " heaven," that is, to the enjoyment of God, as children of his Family, earned by the Blood of the Son. The Christian philosophy of life and literature then is not tame. That excess of power in our hearts, that intensity that rocks the small engine, is met not with a check, but with a call for the expenditure of its every ounce of energy : " Love the Lord thy God with thy whole heart . . . and thy neighbour as thyself."

FAITH

We admit that this is held by faith. It is not a dream. Want of proportion that we can grasp ? What else would be between the Only Being and nothingness come to draw suck of the milk of existence only at the Breast of God. Why then are not all poets Catholic ? First, all truth is partially Christian or wants the complement of Christ. A perception of Christ himself, of Redemption, is not necessary for a pagan poet, but a power of seeing and an appreciation of the interrelation of things is necessary, and possessing this together with the power of words, the pagan poet will be more of a poet than the Christian who is shy, the power of seeing what is under his nose and can only repeat what others say.

GOD, THE SYNTHESIS

In such notes as the preceding, concerned with the nature of the beautiful, the difficulty seems acute, which indeed confronts all our knowledge. The definition, on which that of beauty and all other definitions depend, is that of being, and that we cannot define. Anything has an indefinite number of relationships to everything else, and we do not comprehend the scheme of things. Nor can we know all the processes by which we reach these things. Relations meet us in all knowledge and there is no harder study. We Christians would put the difficulty thus : Creation was the other way about from knowledge, not a laborious ascent from the comparatively unreal. Being is ultimately identified with Actuality, with Goodness, with Beauty, where in the perfect sense they exist, and man knows that only in faith from the words of the Word of God. No poet nor critic but Jesus Christ alone had the beatific vision. No word makes complete sense until we know God. And it seems so foolish, so impertinent to attempt to talk about the Maker of us all, the Only Real, and yet necessary to try. Every study is, truly speaking, practical, which is no more to say than that it is connected with actual truth, with existence ; we want to know where we are and why, and this leads us emphatically through Christ to God. It is by the gift of His Son we know what the Eternal

Father meant by creation. " In this we have known the charity of God because He has laid down He life for us." He, Who came down as rain upon a fleece, as a still wind in the middle of the night, is then the union of His creation. All things are one in Him. He is the secret of the universe that Poetry would utter.

THE EUCHARIST UNIFIES OUR LIFE

There is in our midst a Thing, plain, real, the mystery of mysteries, seen, yet known only by faith, the Holy Eucharist. Its fruit is the union of men with Christ in the Church and so with other men, the renovation of God's creative plan imitating Himself. Plainness and wonder ! They are what make the poet and they are at the centre of all in the Eucharist. Christ and the Holy Spirit come and work from within us, each individual. This work is unlike any other action. It alone recognizes with full comfort the plain truth. To-day especially we are rightly in all fields of endeavour so engrossed in the sociological, I am afraid we may neglect the individual, who is at the bottom of it all. The Eucharist unites that individual with the integral Christ, while preserving his individuality intact. From a consideration of the sacrament in the Sacrifice we might derive all the principles of art. It is something real as the wheatfields and vines that grow from soil and air, sun and rain. It is a sign, it is great, it is a mystery, it is founded in pain, it requires faith.

THE SACRAMENTS AND POETRY

The sacraments are immeasurably superior to all poetry in this, that they effect grace. They are things, not mere " words, words, words," though words have force in them manifesting the great action of the will. The sacraments are real. They act. The Holy Spirit, who works directly in the soul, also works through things we know. A poem dimly resembles the sacraments in this, that it is also an attempt to portray things, active things in a real way. Moreover, the sacraments are signs. Our words too are signs to symbolize, finally, not a general statement of truth, but rather things in act, in which truth ultimately resides. Thirdly, poetry unites the lower creation, soil, air, rain, plant, animal with truth in man, in God. Christ the Word of God, the Son of Man, does this. His sacraments do it. Poetry, in a way far less important than the supernatural sacraments, does it. Rather than say that the sacraments are poetry, I would say that they are the great making, of which poetry might tell were its voice not too weak, had not already the perfect poetry been said with action in their institution. . . . Old Adam is buried in baptism. The new Adam is born because baptism contains the implicit desire of the Eucharist. That representation of the Passion of Christ, the Eucharist forms the Church in Holy Communion, whereby, as grains of wheat form one bread, so our souls and therefore we, by our partaking of the Flesh of Christ Jesus, are joined with Christ. In the corporate body thus formed are the organization and activity necessary to life. But here is the source of life and growth, here the chief work too of the Church, the Mass. What place has this in a treatise on Poetry? Why, this is the central fact that permeates all reality.

THE CHURCH

The Church of Christ, with such weak human limbs as all can see, yet is the fulness and complement, as it were, of Christ, the Word of God. She possesses Him as Head and Heart, and the Spirit He sends forth is her animating Spirit. The Spirit of Love working and moving within the universe of mud and men? There is no other thought so great, so real, so matter of fact, so humbling.

THE CHURCH AND COMMON THINGS

All the common things we know point to the Church of God as to their centre of focus and fulfilment. Look out of the window of the eye. Universe or snowflake tells the free mind it should say there is an Intelligence. If an Intelligence, a Word, and the fulness of that Word is the Church. And no other word has come from God.

THE CHURCH, A VISIBLE THING

This City of God is visible. Every year many find her. Of course, as great writers have pointed out, we cannot investigate even a possible Maker and his message as if He were an equal or his Word just another phenomenon. This is clear when we attempt to realize what a God means, the Maker of every fibre of my being, Who is everywhere and necessary for every bit of existence, life and motion. The help of God is obviously needed.

THE CHURCH, A GROWING THING

This Church is a living part of the life around us. She is an organism, alive, for the Spirit animates and vivifies the Church of Christ. Because of that Spirit she is a growing thing, growing not merely in cold numbers but in her real fulness, which is goodness. Any one, who attempts to realize what paganism was, should admit that the Christian Church has already to a degree converted mankind. The round head of the world has new ideas in it these last two thousand years. And the history of those two thousand years seems to show that the Holy Spirit has caused the Church to grow steadily and, from her beginning to the present day, to increase in numbers relative to the world's population and in her effect upon mankind, in the aggregate sanctity of her members. There is hope in this for the future.

SUMMARY

The tendency to union in all things, which prompts those words of ours we call poetry, appears to me then to be explained and fulfilled only in God, in the substantial Word of God and in the fulness of that Word.

In saying this am I contributing to any of those outlooks thriving in the world of letters that put us in an atmosphere of pseudo-spirituality? No, the real life of faith is built on men being naturally just as poor as they are. Faith tells us that God does good and man also, by the power of and in the love of God.

Neither is this chapter intended to serve as an apology for " Catholic poets." Titles do not make poems. Nor will any philosophy of life suffice. I am trying to say in what that interrelation of things consists, which interrelation is, to my mind, the material of poetry.

XIII

WHETHER THIS EXERCISE OF POETRY SHOULD HAVE A PLACE IN EDUCATION

WE have already suggested that poetry may stand for imaginative study and expression in words. This consideration is concerned with the place of such imaginative exercise in what we call a liberal education. We might put the burden of the present thought in this proposition: that poetry can and should be taught.

MODES OF STUDY

This exercise of the imagination we call poetry should have a part in a general education, that is, in such education as, whether preliminary or prolonged, is supposed to perfect the human faculties or powers for use in the rest of life. Let us attempt a rehearsal of such main facts as are commonly believed with regard to what is called a general education. Naturally we are not treating here of the attainment of some instrument or other of learning, such as rudimentary knowledge of a language. There remain three modes of study generally in practice: first, the gathering of facts or evidence; secondly, mental division, explanation and synthesis; thirdly, imaginative study of things as they appear in life complete and whole. Without at all claiming any particular rank for imaginative work, we think it deserves great attention in any scheme of cultural training.

THE MIND GROWS WITH INCREASE IN POSSESSION

Frequently one hears that any form of teaching should

be inspirational. This is true. But let us for a moment make a more tangible examination of the process of instruction in general. There is more needed than to inspire the pupil. Information is an integral factor, while at the same time all are agreed education is more than a mere accumulation of information. Education is to develop the student's own powers. And such powers grow and are developed by exercise upon the mental food offered them. For instance, in imaginative study the imaginative power or capability is developed by what we store that faculty with, provided the mind absorbs such provender. We should fill the mind with great literature because our human mind exercises and strengthens its powers on food, on what we receive and take into it.

THE IMAGINATION AND CONTACT WITH REALITY

The human mind seeks truth, ultimately ontological truth, outdoor truth, if I may use the phrase. An education that does not exercise the power of realization is apt to dwarf the power of the mind to reach reality. Just as there is the inferior type of the logical mind, which, because of exclusive devotion to logic, knows the answers without having realized the problem, so too there is the reader of the classics of literature, who knows and has read them, but not with comprehension. He knows parrot-like twists of phrase, but rarely exercises the power of realization.

IMAGINATION AND INTELLECTUAL BLINDNESS

Imaginative study is of great importance in education. We should exercise and develop the imagination because that faculty aids us so much in the ascertainment of truth. We can readily see that in our search for truth we must exercise this imaginative power, if we consider how all knowledge starts from things we see, how imagination is built upon observation. For instance, we know people largely from their appearance and action. But often we look at the visible world without attention, without seeing as it were. And more often we glance, or even stare, without realizing what we see. Again we might grant the necessity of realization, if we paused to reflect how little of our thinking in the course of the years is really our own, how much a repetition of formulæ untested by our own acquaintance with reality. And again, without constant return to what we can see, how easy, through a sequence of symbols, to travel mentally far from the truth. We are apt to keep the mind, as it were, like a scholar in a room with the blinds drawn when it would be so profitable to look out through the open window. The habit of realization helps open-mindedness. We will be content to wait for the next peak on our road instead of assuming that we know it all now. Faced with the mystery of things we accept it.

THE IMAGINATIVE MEMORY

If education be a development of the powers of man to enable him to live more fully afterward, then the imagination should have its share, and the memory ; not only the note-taking memory but the imaginative memory of sound and picture, the memory such as an actor has, with gesture and action, of lines. Just as evidence, complete before the mind's eye, assists us to reason correctly, so too words and rhythms in the ear are of prime import in that *exercise*, that activity we know as reading or writing literature.

ATROPHY OF IMAGINATION

The imagination should be given opportunity to grow. Sometimes we speak of imagination as if it were the exclusive possession of childhood and youth. But Shakespeare, the child, did not have the imagination of Shakespeare, the man. The imagination becomes atrophied when, due to immersion in artificial realities, we first refuse to look at fundamental things and then permit the faculty hardly any exercise.

CAN POETRY BE TAUGHT?

But can poetry be taught? As a help to answering this question I offer for consideration some reflections on art and the poet. Remember we asked what sort of a creature is the poet, and we answered he is, first of all, a man, just as any of the rest of us. Everyone is, to a degree, a poet. The poet uses, not occult powers, but his whole self with the sum of all the information it possesses actively at any given time. He must study the art of poetry. Lastly, what makes poetry possible is that in all this plainness, all this dustiness of things, there is obviously cause for wonder and affection. The root of this is that we are all united and capable of further union, yet remaining really distinct individuals. It follows then that poetry can be taught as well as philosophy can be taught. That poetry is of this earth, a gloriously ordinary and usual part of life.

POETRY AN ART, AND MORE

Poetry, we are told, is an art. It is, then, a joining together of materials. This implies work, practice, adjustment. An art admits continued perfectibility. Art calls for workmanship which admits rules and limitations caused by the nature of the material. It implies incidentally that the great principle of criticism of the work, as art, will be : is the piece of work one, and how do the parts contribute to constitute this particular unity? This is not necessarily the complete criticism of the work as literature ; for any use of words must transcend the category of art.

ART AND PLAIN LIFE

Art is a function of ordinary life. We all want music, buildings, stories as much as meat and drink. This in no way derogates from its worth. The joyous contemplation of reality, such recreation is to be our lot in heaven. If beauty be co-extensive with being, with reality as capable of pleasing the beholder, we will expect the pleasure derived therefrom to be as broad as being, restricted of course, according to the perceiving faculty, I mean the power of apprehension or vision, *i.e.*, of intellect and imagination, considering those two as working together. Or, if our interpretation of existence is in terms of human life, if man holds the centre of our stage, if poetry be an imitation of men acting, then the art of poetry will be something as plain as living. The pleasure of art founded in the desire for more life, vicarious great and full life, is generically the pleasure of life.

ART AND UTILITY

I had, up till now, rather avoided the words : " art—useful and fine." With probability, art, etymologically, and therefore, originally, conveyed the idea of the fitting of parts to a whole. From this follows the law of practice in art. For fitting parts to form a whole indicates a medium whether clay, words, sounds, or steps, pigment, etc., and therefore practice according to canons or standards that are expressions of the known possible ways of attaining such results with such substantial media of expression. But, as for utility contrasted with elegance, really music seems just as useful as shoes, even more, if you are looking to a utility that is human.

POETRY MORE THAN ART

Art is such a generic and inclusive term. Poems are after all in the word, the form men use for communication. Language cannot be reduced entirely to the same category as temple building and shoemaking.

THE POET AND LEISURE

But must a poet study the art of poetry? What sort of a creature is the poet? Every man is in degree a poet. Every man has within him something of a poet, otherwise poets would not be read. A good poet will frequent the market place, but he must keep his eyes undimmed. Therefore let him occasionally dwell on one point until his soul be satisfied. Let him lie under a tree and look upward or look out the window and watch the mole scurry under the ivy or periwinkle, let him ask himself, what do I really and honestly see. I do not mean that he should be a poseur, nor worse, a double character, but an ordinary man, which most men have not time to be.

THE POET'S KNOWLEDGE AND HIS POETRY

The poet is not a sensitized plate nor a spinal column. That all intelligent activity, the substance of a man's mental experience, enters transmuted into his poetry has been abundantly proved by Lowes in " The Road to Xanadu." Note in Shelley's " Skylark " or in the magnificent " West Wind " how Shelley's hectic physical desire for freedom appears and the substitution of sensibility for spirituality, which was part of the poet's own mental make-up. I do not mean that you must know a poet's life before reading his poetry. Rather his poetry will give you something of his mental life. The common life of mankind, you might interpose, appears in the pages of the great masters of poetry. But this common or universal life was none the less the poet's. A. E. Housman tells us his poetry comes to him. His knowledge of the Classics, though, and of the elementary meanings, which words had when they stood for visible things, is manifested in every succession of liquid little words. Indeed we might playfully say there is no potency without previous, nay, without present act. The rock has no capacity for hitting me without the strain of lifting and release. And as regards the human head, it is only what is active in one's brain that will find expression. Radiating activity is the only potency.

STUDY NECESSARY FOR RHYTHM

To be a poet one must have read or heard much, for he will need not only pictures in his imagination but words and rhythm. In conceiving poetry the whole mind, intellect and imagination work together. For its concept is not an abstraction but of real things " embodied." With feeling sympathy to form a line then, that suggests what you see, you need an imagination that has already felt the impact of many words in rhythms of phrase, line, and outpouring stream. Note the difference in the meaning of words to us after extensive reading. The word comes freighted not only with " literary allusions " but with the meaning it should have, imaginative meaning. " The earth " does not mean a globe, but this round of struggling soil of ours dwelt on with tragedy.

POETRY AN EXERCISE

There are, to divide roughly, studies where we acquire an instrument, a language for instance ; then there are those in which we scientifically gather, select, and arrange information. There is a third type, carpentry for example, where we exercise ourselves in making something from

G 2

the materials at hand, and where therefore the imagination is exercised. Poetry is one of this type. Even to become a reader of poetry we must try to write it, just as to become a critic of painting we should have to try our hand with pencil and brush. Upon examination it becomes clear that the three types of studies overlap. Again, upon examination of the third type in this simple category, what the rules of composition in literature considered as an art mean becomes clearer. In practical work we do not discard the benefits of past experience just as we do not accept them as commandments.

THE POET A WORKMAN

The poet must be at times a workman in composition, a workman, honest, humble and eager. His work will not be perfect but then neither are his conceptions. He must be willing to practise, to learn his wants, the imperfection of his concepts. Practice, in view of an ideal, will teach the words to come quickly, abundantly, and in just the order they should, even though in a collocation never heard before, just as only exercise will give the facility to invent new steps, to balance on strange ground. By dint of previous practice will the power come in some later moment to imagine with grace or to say spontaneously. Remote labour is behind all the lines that just come to a master poet. There is often immediate toil, as in the case of Vergil "licking his poems into shape." As A. E. Housman indicates, the laboured type of line is frequently not so happy in result as are those lines that form, perfect in the mind, either at the moment of realization or when a master poet lets the music of words flow. But to do this, he has to have an imagination formed in melody by much exercise. Let us put out of our heads the notion that the well-known poets did not study their craft. Take those Romantic poets we consider as most surely of the inspired type. Why do you find in their work exercises in the Rime Royal, Ottava Rima and in almost every other imaginable stanza?

THIS ENHANCES THE VALUE OF POETRY

It may seem paradoxical, but art assumes a not less but more important position in the daily round of life, when we regard the artists, not as mysterious figures, prophets, seers, but as good workmen. Chaucer's stories or Shakespeare's plays should be relished as good tales, admittedly not perfect, if we are to appreciate the human energy and workmanship that went into their making.

TECHNIQUE

Sincerity in expression requires mastered technique. Millions besides Chaucer have seen and heard the coming in of April. More than we think have felt and possessed it as deeply as he, perhaps more deeply. Then why is it the likes of that first score of lines of the Canterbury tales are so very scarce?—when so many have tried? The mind's delight in vision shouts to be expressed. Accurate, realistic expression of things seen must of necessity have definiteness of form, unity, rhythm, because things themselves have that unity we have spoken of, a single harmonic build. The following iambs, the steady change of rhymes knitting Dante's cantos indicate, crudely because humanly, the actual interlocking in one whole cloth of all things, the singleness that we only half perceive. As far as work fails in this indication, in unity, in rhythm, so far it is inexact, so far not true, not honest. To be sincere then, the writer must master control of word, phrase, structure, metric, or not write, content himself with an inarticulate cry, with the lift of the heart. We know the hundreds of pages of Coleridge's indifferent verse, the pile of prose work, the unbelievable heap of reading, but without them we never would have had three real pieces of master work. Here is the magic of Rhythm caught in two dozen plain words :—

> " The moving moon went up the sky,
> And nowhere did abide ;
> Softly she was going up,
> And a star or two beside."

That " air of careless growth " in the best of Blake is not at all unpremeditated. Blake was careful, meticulous, hard working. The fresh and unearthy music echoes out of brooding and sweat. It is the intellect, labouring intellect, that welds the sight seen, the sound heard into an unfading something rich and strange.

RHYTHM ESSENTIAL

I have admitted these words concerning rhythm into a book devoted to the nature of poetry, because I believe we cannot know poetry without intimate knowledge of rhythm. It is of the very fabric of any flow of language that can be called literature. It is part of such portrayal of the real as literature attempts. We used to quarrel about the necessity of metre, but to say that some form of rhythm is too external or non-essential to enter into the definition of literature would be as if one should say the body is too external a thing to be an essential constituent of man. And poetry is a human piece of work, not angelic.

ART DONE TO ORDER

It is no denial of inspiration to admit that many of the greatest works of art were done to order. As for student work, in class after class, I have found the best work in

English came in prescribed sonnet form, the worst when the men were left free.

WORK AND INSPIRATION

The student scribbling verses scruples over his labour in versification, feeling it a denial of inspiration. He forgets that poetry is work in a definite medium, just as much as is the composition of music. Should the beginner sacrifice truth to rhyme? He should not lie in order to rhyme. But perhaps he will have to wait a long time before he can put in verse such subtle truth as that of Hamlet.

THE READER MUST WORK

Now, if in following the poet's vision, the reader exercises himself in a way similar to that of the poet, this reader works then in order to achieve the enjoyment of poetry of great beauty. The pleasure of surveying the world from a mountain peak, around which the winds of the world are blowing, calls for more effort than is needed to lift a stein in the inn on the valley floor.

THE LITERARY TYPE?

Perhaps the one excuse for this unprofessional essay, which will save it from being just another and therefore unnecessary book concerning the nature of literature, lies in this, that it does not admit the existence of the literary type. Story-tellers, yes, there are such men. And again all men at times try to grasp real knowledge. The language of knowledge of the real as distinct from the expression of symbols in abstraction and precision, that is literature, is it not? But all men practise that. Why do we still insist that poets are strange creatures or poetry a weird phenomenon, when they and it are most human? Something comes to the poet from the outside. He must awake and see, that is true, but why from that assume that the poet is a characterless plate for impressions? Historically recognized poets seem to have had very definite characters. Why do we perpetuate the hoary tradition that the poet is an empty vessel, uninteresting on weekdays? Less interesting than the rest of us? I wish Plato had not started that.

If the reader of poetry does in a lesser way what the poet has done, if art is work and the poet a worker, then we can learn in a humble degree to appreciate and exercise the art of the poet.

In the consideration that is ending we have discussed imaginative study in education without refining these terms beyond their generally accepted values. But in our next consideration we might go further and ask: Is education in literature interpretative of human life, and is imaginative study, therefore, primarily a study of man?

XIV

IF THE STUDY OF LITERATURE BE AN INTIMATE STUDY OF THE STORY OF MAN

POETRY INTERPRETATIVE OF HUMAN LIFE

> " We are such stuff
> As dreams are made on, and our little life
> Is rounded with a sleep."

Do these lines from " The Tempest " interpret human life, and not those others, which run :

> " Full fathom five thy father lies ;
>   Of his bones are coral made :
> Those are pearls that were his eyes :
>   Nothing of him that doth fade,
> But doth suffer a sea-change
> Into something rich and strange.
> Sea-nymphs hourly ring his knell ;
> Hark ! now I hear them,—ding-dong, bell."

Poetry that is content with picturing can yet speak, it would seem, most eloquently of life and death and change.

NOT ONLY THEORETICAL POETRY

Or, on a larger scale, is the " De Rerum Natura " of Lucretius and the theoretical second part of Goethe's " Faust " and the work of those poets, who, to-day tackle the sociological and economic problem of our time, are these to be regarded as views and interpretations of life, partial or complete, while poetry that rests with portrayal and voices no theory is not so to be regarded ?

Let us call in evidence the picture Maurya gives of her aged self at the burial of her last son in " Riders To The Sea " by John Synge :

" It's a great rest I'll have now, and great sleeping in the long nights after Samhain, if it's only a bit of wet flour we do have to eat and maybe a fish that would be stinking."

What more penetrating commentary on the human soul could be desired than these words from the tired heart itself ? This passage is more illuminating than any amount of analysis of ineradicable self-interest or of the wearing effect of time and emotion. Witness the picture created from their own mouths, of the chorus of women in " Murder in the Cathedral " by T. S. Eliot, the picture which begins :

> " We have not been happy, my Lord, we have not been
> too happy."

Witness such an evidently and richly imaginative play as " Macbeth."

EVEN THE LIGHTER LYRICS

Not only the multitude of lyrics, which deplore mortality, such as Herrick's " To Daffodils," but even such a purely lyrical piece as Shakespeare's :

> " Hark ! hark ! the lark at heaven's gate sings,
> And Phœbus 'gins arise,
> His steeds to water at those springs
> On chalic'd flowers that lies ;
> And winking Mary-buds begin
> To ope their golden eyes :
> With every thing that pretty is,
> My lady sweet, arise :
> Arise, arise ! "

offers a view of life, does it not, although but a partial

and momentary one. It is not, to be sure, as philosophical as the great moving-picture, which made a Nietzschean conflict of Night and Day out of Bottom's play.

POETRY SOMETHING OF A TEACHER

All that comes in contact with us, all life, teaches, but is not poetry closer to formal education than random experience ? Poetry is imaginative, not abstract, yet, by the very fact that it picks for its picture those details from nature which form an impression, it interprets nature. A poem narrows the focus of our view. Poetry, furthermore, seeks to voice essentials. Lastly, poetry is vocal, a groping effort to see on the part of the human mind. For these reasons I would conclude that all poetry is interpretative. How could a man portray life and omit the puzzle of good and evil, omit change and mortality ?

THE FUNDAMENTAL LESSON

Horace gives us the key. To quote from one of his permanent lyrics on " Spring and Death " : here is Horace describing the passage of the seasons :

" Damna tamen celeres reparant caelestia lunae :
       Nos, ubi decidimus
Quo Pater Aeneas, quo dives Tullus et Ancus
       Pulvis et umbra sumus.
Yet the swift moons repair the losses in the skies :
       We, when we have fallen
Where Father Aeneas, where rich Tullus and Ancus lie,
       Are dust and shadow."

POETRY NOT THEREBY ENFEEBLED

Poetry that concerns itself with the fundamental or general view of human life is apt to dwell on the transitoriness of existence. I do not mean that, for that reason, poetry has to be mournful and wan. There is plenty of virility in :

"For they're hanging Danny Deever in the morning."—

or in

"All thy friends are lapped in lead."—

or in

"Awake ! for morning in the bowl of night
Has flung the stone that puts the stars to flight."

The very versification in the mediæval lyrics is suggestive of vitality. Let me instance a stanza from a thirteenth century manuscript, quoted in Helen Waddell's "Mediæval Latin Lyrics" :

"De ramis cadunt folia,
nam viror totus periit,
iam calor liquit omnia
et abiit ;
nam signa coeli ultima
sol petiit."

Here is Helen Waddell's lovely translation :

"Down from the branches fall the leaves,
A wanness comes on all the trees,
The summer's done ;
And into his last house in heaven
Now goes the sun."

I cannot quote from mediæval love poetry without adding one brief example from the greater verse of the hymns, whence perhaps the buoyancy and manliness of the verse of the lyrics of those centuries is derived. Surely a martial note enters into that hymn of "Fortunatus to the Cross," which begins : "The standards of the King advance" :

"Vexilla regis prodeunt :
Fulget crucis mysterium,"—

These verses certainly offer a definite view of life and pain. But it is time I resumed discussion of the relation of poetry to education.

Human life needs interpretation: raw experience without interpretation produces pain without wisdom. Now, literature is obviously a part and a record of human life. But it is both less and more than a complete stenographic record. It is a study.

Before considering the proposal that imaginative study is primarily a study of man, it seems proper to entertain thought of the interpretative nature of education. Should that section of the years we devote to liberal or non-vocational education be consecrated ultimately to an interpretation of life?

Education is more than an indefinite development of the powers of the student, since this development itself clearly must take place along with and through growth in learning and wisdom. The student's capacity or ability, if it is to exist at all, cannot remain formless. So education while painstakingly objective, while not reckoning beyond the evidence, should teach, should, in an ideal State, interpret and interpret truly, the meaning of life. Is not a general or liberal education, such education as fits us for the general task of living more fully human lives, of using our nature's fullest capacities, is not such education itself primarily concerned with a study of man and the life of man?

EDUCATION NOT A MATTER OF ANSWERS

When I say that education should furnish an interpretation of life, I do not mean that education can or should give complete answers and so induce that habit of mind that quotes the answer without realization of problem or answer. Education in poetry, as in every study, should look forward to and ensure a succeeding growth. We can hardly appreciate the texture of a great poem without maturity. And, in general, when the clouds of experience rain down in later life, such storms will submerge the conclusions of youth, they cannot drown a living growth of thought. Destructive of intellectual leadership and growth in a commonwealth is the effect of learning a few principles of literature or science or philosophy with the feeling that that is all there is to be learned. The college, it is true, should not be just a preparation for the university, but it should be a preparation for further intellectual development.

ANY SYSTEM OF EDUCATION A GROWTH

No individual ever fully constructed a system of education. Such systems are a growth. And they grow from the desire to answer this question : what are we, and what is our life ? Is not this the study of our whole lives ? I ask the question because it seems to me that the same study, which, by natural circumstance and tendency, is the main study of our lives, is, as a matter of fact, also the chief study of formal education. The obvious question we ask in life is : Where and why am I ? What is man ? Then this is the question in school too.

EDUCATION RELIGIOUS

I would like to be diplomatic, to enter through the adversary's door. But the first fact about every system of education in time and the first quality determining its character is that it was, and is, of its nature, religious. I do not say : " should be religious." Education is religious. Like drama, and I suppose barter for that matter, education took its origins everywhere in religion. Even American colleges were originally seminaries.

—NATURALLY SO

What else could education do ? All study is practical. The most abstruse problem of astronomical mathematics is intended to help solve the one great curiosity of humankind ; where and why are we, what is this life, what for ? . . . And where are we men ? Why, here on earth. All other words seem vain set side by this sober phrase. We breathe this air, we are fed and clothed by this earth, we never leave it, we are bone of its bone and flesh of its elements. We are here with men. Our main concern is man. He is ourselves, our life ; our words are of his life, but of his life on earth. " All of us feed by gift of earth " and " are the saddest of the beasts of the field." In our very view of the material world, what is our great concern ? To determine what and why we are. All studies are bound up ultimately with this or, in other words, all study is a study of God in terms of his work, man.

LITERATURE TEACHES

The stories of literature, although written of individuals in particular circumstances, will be stories of universal appeal to us of the audience, stories, as it were, concerned with life itself. They will have this universal note because of the relation men bear to one another in the human family. These stories, since they deal, in a sense, with the life of all of us, its fundamental needs, emotions and aspirations, will teach some views or other of life and living. Literature does teach persistently. We are perhaps too apt to abuse our power of analysis by pigeonholing in separate tight compartments studies and operations that will not stay so conveniently separate. Christianity for instance was taught through the story

of Luke, the epistles of Paul and the sermons of Chrysostom before ever it was put in thesis form.

LITERATURE, THE STUDY OF MAN

The great object of imaginative study is man and his
world, his environment. It is the study of human nature,
this inevitably, because man and his world are what we
will meet with, the object and terminology of our knowledge. This imaginative study of man in order to be
imaginative must be, not of human nature in the abstract,
but of men, of individuals. This study of man is of man
as he is, as he gazes at mountains or burrows in cities,
as he talks or deals with other men and, most important
of all, as he is the creature, image and child of God, from
God and bound to God, in Him moving and living and
having his being. Men in conversation and in books
preoccupy themselves with this last relation, which also
pervades the other two.

LITERATURE NOT ANALYSIS

The study, if imaginative, is precisely of what the
individual does in marked circumstance. While keeping
then the common traits of human nature in main view, a
particular people together with the ideas that dominated
their conduct and institutions should be studied through
the literature of that same people, precisely because we
are studying men, not an abstract. Imaginative study is
necessary because analysis alone will not suffice. Under
even a mental dissection man, when we break him apart,
ceases to be alive. Such study is to be done as far as
possible, in the imaginative way. What did Euripides
see on the Acropolis and below it? What was there for
him to read before he wrote the plays? Picture from
the writings left by the Greeks themselves the heritage

of sound freedom, heroism, healthy inquiry, slavery, open-air quarrelling, peculation and defeat that left Demosthenes' Athenians incapable of action.

LITERATURE A HISTORY?

The imagination must study man through men. But let us not forget its proper study is rather man than facts or data. This imaginative study aims at knowledge of the heart of man and is concerned with fact finding only as a help to an honest view of man. If we borrow the word "history" for use in this chapter, we do it somewhat, as in an earlier consideration, we borrowed "picture." By history here we mean rather the imaginative picture of man in action, the real story of mankind in so far as we can come by it.

CONTENT AND STYLE NOT TO BE SEPARATED

Some may object: "stuff and nonsense! The Freshman and Sophomore years in literature should be devoted to a study of style." Would we then be in the midst of a "content *versus* style" controversy? There is something of a reconciliation is there not in this, that you can't have a true study of one without the other? Correct style flows from content. As Cicero, who in a sense has bequeathed our various languages to us, puts it: "The power of saying belongs to no one who has not taken possession of that which he would say. Dicendi enim virtus nisi ei, qui dicet, ea, quae dicet, percepta sunt exstare non potest" ("De Oratore, 48"). Nay more, there is mutual interdependence; imaginative thought even presupposes words, melody, and picture. We cannot even conceive individual imaginative objects properly without words and pictures. One instance of this latter point: how do we normally judge a new acquaintance? To ourselves we say something like this : " He is like Brown in his strutting walk ; Smith, in that narrowing of the eyes ; I would be afraid he would do so and so in certain circumstances like the man I have forgotten ; he reminds me of Jones in the way he reacts when questioned." We do not, often could not, say he is ambitious, kindly, etc.

Without constant attention to the matter, the thought, we should have a study of elegance in the worst meaning of the word, of style abhorring thought. On the other hand without constant attention to the words and their order, we should have a bare analysis of the thought, which in poetry misses the very point since such analysis is not a study of things as such, but of ideas. Nothing of what has just been said is meant to identify either the object of the artist's portrayal or the full state of soul of the artist with the limited form finally selected for communication. But while not identical, thought and style are inseparable. The question of style is : does the man convey, as nearly as he can with arbitrary symbols, what the whole man, not a floating intellect, wants to express ? I said " convey," because language of its nature is communicative. The most difficult of poets wants at least a reader or two.

THE EMPHASIS IMPORTANT

In much great authorship, the concentration was not upon writing literature. In all great authorship it certainly was on truth. I am not against teaching correctness of style. Because we are teaching men, living units, all the debated methods of pedagogy are of use in any year in school. The distinctions are of emphasis. But the emphasis is important. I think a study of style and study of thought must go together, and that the main emphasis, if your student is capable, should be on thought. He will be capable if circumstances started him thinking at an early age, for we are the creatures of that gift of God, environment. If your student is not capable, even then the shortest way to what he can achieve will be through a study of truth working out to style.

In learning to drive a car, the stage must come early where the direct attention is no longer on the shifting of each gear but is concerned with proceeding to a certain place. So in walking; so in all matters of exercise and practice; so I think, in the study of style, once the rudiments of grammar have been absorbed, the student reader should concentrate on what Cicero or Matthew Arnold is trying to tell us in particular circumstance. Just so in composition, which should, of course, be plentiful, the student writer's direct attention should be on what he has to say.

THE REAL QUESTION

The phrase " content *versus* style " does not seem quite fair. For the advocates of a study of style certainly desire that students should be trained to think and to consider the ideas, to see the picture, behind the expression. The divergence between the two groups seems rather to be in their answers to the question: " What sort of thought should be emphasized? Rhetorical theme and argument or study and contemplation of man and his earth? " All would agree that, to practice or achieve style, the student must understand the thought. The real question is: With what sort of understanding? Mainly of device, or of the things the words tell about, man and nature? Poetic study must be imaginative—and poetry is a word about things.

So there remains the question: Has the enjoyment of literature as such, distinguished from grammar, rhetoric and scientific philology, any place in a classroom at all ? To-day a question interests those educators who have a tradition : Is this study of literature in schools to be a training of schoolboys in expression—should they merely learn from Cicero how to plead, from Juvenal how to satirize—or is it an exercise in imaginative reconstruction, from the words of the ancients, a sympathetic understanding, of the minds of the past ? Practice and precedent seem to offer ammunition to those who make composition the direct goal. Personally, I believe with the others that literature, even in school, should be a more intimate study of the story of man than formal history of fact can be, a study of history from the words of a people themselves, from the inside as it were, and that this is most important even in producing powers of correct expression.

THE POWER OF EXPRESSION

Even if we wished the study of letters to confine itself to the production of the perfect orator, the man capable of self-expression, such an aim in itself implies much more than its phraseology explicitly states. For perfected power of expression depends upon highly developed imaginative power. Now, the imagination's function is to keep us in touch with reality. Without the habit of realization, expression becomes a repetition of borrowed sayings. Without realization, oratorical sincerity will be wanting because such contact with reality is lacking as would make the orator's own that view of life he will offer others in his speech.

I think all, or almost all, would agree that the entire purpose of literary study as at present understood is not summed up in the laudable ambition to produce polished expression. Putting aside then for the moment this practical and praiseworthy aim of classes in rhetoric and composition, and rather asking what other ends may be achieved in literary study, we find that one rough way of determining the purpose of collegiate classes in literature would be to say that they attempt to answer the question : " Why read literature, stories or poems, in or out of schools ? " To define the value we should seek in books, this is much the same as to ask : " What is literature ? " The answer appears in the course of years of reading, since reading books with imagination is an exercise, wherein attainment is achieved only by practice.

LITERATURE AND LIBERAL EDUCATION

The question " Why read books ? " might be a partial substitute for the query " What is a liberal education ? " " How does it differ from specialized education ? " For, while mathematics and many other studies are parts in such education, the imaginative study of literature, if it belongs to education at all, has, alone of all studies, place in a general education and nowhere else. Biology and chemistry one must know to become a doctor, rhetoric in order to plead or preach, philology to be a teacher of literature, mathematics and mechanics before qualifying as a candidate for engineering ; philosophy and astronomy are specialities as it were ; poetry, treated as poetry, remains the only ingredient in humanistic culture that has no voice in any other classroom than its own. If then poetry as such entertains no special vocational purpose, if its only effort is to make us more fully human, this in itself would cause the surmise that it is primarily a study of man.

THE CLASSICS

I think that we should weigh the position of the

classics. This will not be a wayward digression because so many still esteem the classics as the kernel of literature.

The case for Greek and Latin literature could be summarized thus : (1) All study is a study of God ; (2) therefore of man ; (3) therefore of man in the past as well as in the present ; (4) therefore for us, in the first place, of the Greek and Roman ; (5) therefore of Latin and Greek in the original. Let me explain. (1) All study is to find out what life means, the why and wherefore of it. This is a study of God. (2) To the Christian, man is the image of God. If anything does, he gives glory, is, in a sense, the word of God. However, if you object to this, man and human life are in any case the necessary and inevitable object of our study. (3) To understand the meaning of words we must know history. To understand human life in the present we must understand its growth, what has remained the same, what changes have taken place, what recurrences. (4) For us of Europe and America, Athens and Rome are the origin of our civilization. Our habits and moulds of thought we inherit from them. By origin is not meant that they gave us the rudimentary forms from which our own have evolved, as one might say Beowulf was part of the origins of English. No, we still reason, argue, play, write and govern in the very forms we have inherited from Greeks and from Romans. They were at the cross-roads too, at the start of the unique thing, Christianity. But there is really only one proof of the value of the classics. This they offer of themselves to men who read them. No extrinsic argument is satisfying. It is hardly sufficient even to argue that Homer taught Plato dramatic dialogue, taught Demosthenes directness and all the Greeks literature, the art of the story-teller, and therefore will so teach us. Many years have passed. Finally, at least some of the classics must have to-day intrinsic worth. Finally, Plato and Homer as well as Calderon and Shakespeare must be the best books the poor old world has, portraying better than others the truths of existence, if we are to read them at the early period when we have leisure and assistance. Since proof that reading the classics is worth while will ultimately depend upon some intrinsic good in the classics, and since reading is an exercise, the final proof of the value of such reading cannot be given but by the classics themselves to the man who is reading them. Furthermore, literature, of its nature not a recital of bare facts, but a call to the mind of the reader to realize a real truth, tells its imaginative message with just the right amount and kind of symbol and sound. Then to tell the same message, I can only repeat the classics. (5) In the original, first from the nature of poetry, of style and of translation ; translation necessarily changes, adds or leaves out. We cannot imaginatively enter the mind of Plato or Cicero through translation, much less of Homer or Horace. Secondly, try it, read the Iliad in English, then in the original, and you will agree. If the classics be a fraud, why does everyone who has read Homer through with poetic realization think that to read the Iliad in Greek is the best lesson in poetry. Is this fair for me to use as an answer ? If literature be an art and therefore a practice, if literature be a matter of realization, it is a fair statement. But don't be afraid that Latin will disappear. As long as it is the language of the Church it will have its place in school. And, as long as Latin remains, Greek will be sought out.

ENGLISH AND OTHER TONGUES

Our poets know other languages than the English, in which they write. Many of them are well acquainted with Greek and Latin. If I were a linguist, I would try to show the peculiar wealth of the English language and literature. For one thing, the body of English lyrics, for another the plays in the English language, exhibit such variety in thought and manner. But this wealth of our tongue is borrowed from many sources. These sources did not cease with the period before 1400. During the centuries subsequent to that date, contributions from the Latin and Greek classics, as well as from more modern literatures, have continued to inflow into the English. What we may call the Latin Mode and the Greek Mode are everywhere in our volumes. But this book is hardly the place to develop this thought. Suffice it to say, that not for nothing did English schoolboys study Demosthenes and Cicero. Consider, further, the riches derived from old French and modern French, from the Italian plots and stanzas. Add to such sources, that the wealth and flexibility of English has been increased by the diversity of life of the peoples who have used it. This life has not been confined to one locality nor to one tradition. The fact that English in the course of a long continuous activity, has been the purveyor of thoughts bred in more than one local tradition is perhaps more important than the sweep of ground the English language covers. Here we might consider that American life has enriched the English language more markedly than would appear from the shelves of American contributions to the English classics. I do not mean to dwell upon the new thoughts, phrasing (at times delicious, at times bad) and vocabulary, derived from Irish, German, Italian and other immigrants. Nor would I emphasize the coining of words for American inventions. Less obviously but none the less really, I believe, the language has gained from a fresh liberty of spirit, existing despite our many petty tyrannies, from an American willingness to learn and to do. Not to drag the case out longer, I will say that the English language may appear like some strange creature that should have borrowed spots and stripes from all the tribes of the forest, it may sprawl at times somewhat shapelessly, but it is a joy to read in it. To enjoy that reading according to its worth, we ought to know something of other languages, because the singular adaptability and expressiveness of English is derived from many other languages and literatures.

LITERATURE AND HISTORY

Not only the ancient classics, but all literature is a more intimate history, a study of history from the inside as it were. Literature helps to an imaginative philosophy of history, so vital in all scholarship. Literature is an imaginative reconstruction of other people and other times. Such knowledge of mankind is gathered from personal life and from the life of the race, as books and tradition give it.

EVERY MAN A MICROGEN

Let us consider the first source, personal life. Each one of us is, not only a microcosm but, if I may coin the word, a microgen, an epitome of the race. If so, on any question one can and should sometimes suspend the process of study and ask himself: what do I feel is the real point, the essential point, honestly, apart from books and cleverness, whether it be brilliant or not, whether it be held by one or be more aptly perhaps the unspoken thought of thousands. This is the way of attaining to that realization we spoke of before. So, too, considering another's position we can consider, how would I act in the environment of this other. Thus dramatization is not the exclusive property of impressionable characters, but is latent in every man as a microgen.

If we are, each of us, an epitome of the human family, then, by the exercise of realization, the individual can appreciate different types of men from himself. If the scholar sees the moment in the past when he owed this or that awakening thought to such and such an influence, he will not think of himself as a superior cast of pottery. Nor will he so easily be thrown off balance by the discovery of morons in an University club.

IMAGINATION AND SPECULATION

There is need of imagination to accompany scientific scholarship and prevent it from becoming dusty and foolish. For instance in historical studies all admit that imaginative reconstruction and dramatic sympathy, provided such be plain and not illusory, will help much to keep the mind from wandering in labyrinths of speculation. The imagination is the power of keeping in touch with reality.

POETRY AND LIBERTY

The worship of human authority will soon cut us all to the pattern of some mechanistic conception. Imagination alone will save us, imagination, which is a grasp of reality, not a flight of unfettered fancy. The philosopher invents Utopia, the poet portrays men and cities.

IMAGINATION AND DISCOVERY

Imagination seems never to have received due attention in education. Its growth is often prevented in education by superimposed layers of cleverness. Imagination, or better, realization, will help produce the proper union between the theoretical and the real, between studies and life. If the coming generation is to produce something new, its members must seek it by looking out the window at the world as it is, for that something will be older than Hegelianism or Platonism, older than all the critical books.

IMAGINATIVE RECONSTRUCTION

Allow me a bit of hurried illustration of what I have called dramatic reconstruction. What a dry enigma Socrates is, if we cannot enter just a bit into the old man's mind, if we cannot imagine the reason for the old man's humour. Or again, " Rome was no larger than Reading," but with the imagination we can see that, if New York were one-tenth its present size, yet the largest, it would still have the same meaning to us. Another example of the want of this test by imagination can be found in the man who reads all life in terms borrowed from books he has learned, forgetting to look at what happens or has happened. Not to take any extreme example of pedantry of such type as is familiar to all students, to discuss Hamlet's mother-fixation has always seemed to me so bookishly Freudian when the play, read with imagination, cries aloud that Hamlet's idol was his father.

IMAGINATION AND THE NORMAL

Imagination that links us to common truth is far different from curious delving into the abnormal. In fact the imagination is apt to see in the abnormal only its essence, for example, the plain badness of a selfish child in a Roman Emperor's irregularities. In the greatest poets realization does not busy herself with the appreciation of every pathological tendency. Note how Shakespeare differs from his contemporaries precisely in this point, that he offers common truths that can move us all.

EDUCATION NOT ANCESTOR-WORSHIP

Cultivation of the historical imagination is the only possible vaccination to prevent our thinking the world started the year we were born. And education should not be ancestor-worship. Tradition is the passing on of a heritage. Reading the history of the world with imagination may keep us from passing on the faults of one generation as if they were the virtues of Methusaleh. And to read the story of mankind with dramatic sympathy or imaginative reconstruction we must review our own lives in the same spirit.

THE STUDY OF MAN FROM WITHIN

This study of the image of God, man, is made, not by a scholar standing apart, but as Christ studied God and man, as part, as belonging to man. From within we reach out in living growth. From within we must study the image of God, man, remembering we are men. Men are not specimens in our laboratories. This will help us to the comprehension of the good in some terms we hear. For one, " leadership." If we belong to man, men are not our instruments. Leadership means mutual help with more reaching out and expansion on the part of him to whom God has given more in some phase or other of life. Teaching, whether in a subway train or classroom (and all language according to St. Augustine is to teach), is the planting of a seed, which, unless it be buried in the ground and die, does not bear fruit. Here two things are important—we plant the seed and it is buried. We plant the seed. Sitting alongside, as it were, looking through the listener's eye, we aim to put the thought as if from within him, due to our kinship in the first and second Adam. The listener and ourselves are sons of one family. We feel and think fundamentally the same thoughts. How much more by the powers of the grace of Christ can we expect agreement with the truth, that the hearer will and can see? Secondly, the seed is buried. The other man makes off unconscious of having been taught. If well taught, he takes the idea as his own. Why? Because you did not teach him. You put before him a symbol, a sign, a *suggestion*. You were not in his mind to do the work. The Holy Spirit and the man himself see and make the thought. He does make it his own. He teaches himself. One is tempted to say you can give a man a new idea, provided it be an old one of his own. More truly the listener does make new ideas part of his old possession. All new thought enters not into a separate pigeonhole, but into relation with all that is active in the body of thought in the mind. What different meanings, for instance, " We must be progressive " has for the constant reader of a Hearst journal and a reader of " The Catholic Worker."

But let us rest from discussion of educational aims and methods. In the fields of wisdom, knowledge and art, there is room for so much to be done. No one has yet written the poetry or music or apologetic or mathematic that should be written. Let us not spend our time in such analysis of art as assumes that God's world is worn out. We have hardly broached the barrels of good wine in the deep cellar.

XV

WHETHER THERE IS ANY INTRINSIC CONNECTION BETWEEN VOLUNTARY ACTIVITY AND REALIZATION

READING AND EXPERIENCE

WE are all so used to books, we fail to notice how much of our life they constitute, how much we have learned, not orally from those we live with, but from books, how many vivid characters we know only in books. Of recurring interest is the thought in general of the interrelation of reading and other more direct experience. The characters and events we meet with in books borrow flesh and blood, poignancy and sharp, acid taste from the more vividly personal experience we suffer outside of literature ; the latter in turn gains in mellow richness and significance from fulness of reading. But the following consideration is concerned more narrowly with the connection between wisdom and voluntary action.

POETRY AND PRACTICAL LIVING

A poem is not an exhortation, but a portrayal. It is to feed us, to give us something rather than to demand something from us. But, since we have only one life to live, we may well ask : " Is there not some vital connection between our imaginative possessions and practical action ? "

In an attempt to indicate a philosophy of literature I feel I have the right to say where I think poetry fits in the scheme of life in general. We might say that we have considered the relation of poetry to theoretical life and that now we could take up its nexus with practical life.

STUDY AND SPIRITUALITY

There is to-day a demand, greater perhaps than for many centuries, for the establishment of an intimate and essential union between studies and the spiritual life of the student. Students want to see how their studies will affect the goodness or happiness of their lives.

REALIZATION AND WISDOM

We might define wisdom as a correct view of life, a view in which knowledge is kept sound by healthy imaginative realization. This, the usual distinction between wisdom and learning is, we must confess, finely drawn because one hardly possesses the real facts without wisdom. Appreciating the paramount importance of conviction, we are thinking here especially of the influence of real knowledge, of realization, upon visible activity. A proposition that Mr. Spifkins admits is less likely to have results than a truth which the gentleman realizes, which has become real to him. Let us break our present consideration into two parts, the first to note how wisdom may influence action, the second how action influences our view of life.

EDUCATION AND ACTION

Education, we have said, should include formation of the habit of realization, of imaginative contact with reality; and again education should interpret life. It follows that education should lead to action. Therefore education should be a living thing as it were, unified and vivified by some inner principle. How can education be impregnated with such a principle of unity and life and yet remain open to any truth that may appear? The aim of education should be to assist man not to the possession of some undigested load upon the mind but to the possession of a power of honest vision, formed by exercise in viewing reality, adaptable to strain and stress, unobscured by concupiscence.

LITERATURE'S THREE VIEWS OF LIFE

The body of literature the world possesses offers roughly three interpretations, each containing some degree of realization of the world in which we live and each with practical consequences affecting our manner of life and conduct.

THE MATERIALISTIC VIEW

The first, the materialistic view is persuasive because founded not only in the war of the body against the spirit so that, if we live it, we believe it, but founded in the root fact of experience. This fact scholastic philosophy stoutly affirms. The material of all experience comes first through the senses. Materialism as an affirmation can't be wrong. But the materialistic proceeds to make the truth he grasps the whole truth. You are so much chemistry. There is no intelligence, nor heart. There is no meaning back of it. Have a good time; but you won't. This is the philosophy of rank materialism, and to thought a blank wall.

THE HUMANISTIC VIEW

The second view is that of the humanist in any age who sees joy in a glint of sunshine, a spring of water, a fugitive friendship; and always along with it death; and holding these ideas in either hand, in between he voices his advice; "Don't throw yourself away; common sense, decorum, control, restraint, measure, the golden mean, nothing too much." But to preserve even the measure of the humanist, the duality of human nature calls for a third power, the Spirit of God. To keep an ordinary human family together in plain comfort requires an extravagant emptying of self.

THE CHRISTIAN VIEW

In the third view, the excess of longing in the human heart is met with and more than adequated by a permission and an encouragement to excess of act—love God without limit, love neighbours as God. This is the philosophy of Christ, of the Catholic Church, expressed again in: "He that shall lose his life shall save it." It aims beyond. It attains happiness even here in so far as it aims beyond here. The doctrine "He that shall lose his life shall save it" is the doctrine of life and of great literature; that material success is failure and material failure success (blended with much inferior life, of course, in any one character, not standing clear) is the truth of life, of Anna Karenina, of Macbeth, of Œdipus. That the doctrine of Christ should be partly enunciated by literature is not strange, since Christ complemented and supplemented man, fallen man. The Realist is true as he preaches that seeming success is failure; the Romantic as he emphasizes that the aim should be expansive and infinite. Here too, if we pause, why there is no bulk of *purely* Christian literature becomes easier to see, when we reflect that the world (I am not thinking on numbers), the spirit of the world, in which Christians live much of their time and to which they devote much of their energy, never has been Christ's. He said it never would be.

MEN ARE OF COMMON STOCK

This philosophy of life holds, as a fundamental truth of human nature, that men are kindred, suffering from a common wound, that everyone of us, even the favoured ego, must admit himself capable of becoming the protagonist in some " Richard III." of his own. The union and quasi-kinship of things we spoke of holds good all the more strongly in the human family. How false seems the division lesser poets make into sweet and sour souls beside the treatment of human character in Hamlet, Macbeth or the Odyssey, where the common weakness and strength of the human soul are revealed. Realization suggests to us, as it shows poet or saint, that we are all of one root, each capable of becoming better or worse. Great tragedy and the universal appreciation of Periclean and Elizabethan tragedy would have been impossible if men were of different kinds. How, in this case, do the glaring differences between sheep and goats arise ? If tragedy holds an ironical mirror up to life, it depicts, along with the bitterness and puzzlement of our lot, the effects of human choice, those slight turns of a man's will, after which the mind itself can be clouded or cleared

—WITH COMMON ILLS

There arises slowly and quietly in the mind of anyone, who has reached a certain maturity and has worked not only with materials but with minds, a conviction that everyone of us is prone to sickness of soul. Glimpse the walled thoughts of a person—what mists enveloping a central growth of intangible hope and fear ! Our troubles are, in the branches so plausible, and at the roots, let us say it with all kindness to ourselves, at the roots they are our worship of self. " What one wants, that he thinks, while the facts are often quite otherwise." We are all apt to become experts in one art, self-deception. We adjust the details around us into a solar system of our own. Thus our faults are always noble. Yet in sober truth every form of sin is mean. All are of the same stock. A tyrant is no less ignoble than the child piercing flies on the windowpane. If one should mirror to himself his real scene, what an uncomfortable figure would show in it. But only the Maker can understand this fellow surely; comfort seeking, swept by what storms of terrible proprietary devotion, capable of heroism. "Ah, for sure an oyster this fellow," but always beneath the shell strange troubles. Each of us can remark " Can such things be and overcome us like a summer's cloud without our special wonder ? "

THOUGHT AND CONDUCT

Such interpretation as we have described, if accompanied by realization, will affect life and conduct. But conduct will affect conviction. There appears a mutual action. Not only does thought prompt to act, our human or moral acts have influence upon our state of mind.

MOTIVE

Writing that is dictated by personal pride or lust or worship of money or hatred or envy will be false, false at least in so far as such given motive force has prevailed. Reproduction of the real presupposes open-eyed fidelity and humility. I cannot believe, no matter how often I hear it, that pride, that inordinately subjective and therefore untrue attitude which spoils everything else in this world, makes the work of the artist. The greatest artists may have been somewhat insufferable before and after the good work was done, but in the creative act they must have been receptive and patient.

This consideration does not for a moment imply that François Villon was not a poet. The question is rather, other things being equal, does there not seem to be some natural and intrinsic connection between will and wisdom ?

THE DREAMER

I have never thought of the poet as but a dreamer. For the poet must first see things as they are. And dreaming divorced from action will sooner or later cease to consist of true dreams.

WISDOM AND GOODNESS

Wisdom demands a good life. We might as well face the truth. Act against your thought, the thought will sooner or later be forgotten. Particularly is this true if the thought were imaginative, a sight of something. Habits of thought demand habits of action based on such thought, if the thoughts are to endure. In experience we have all been made aware that selfish interests cloud the judgment, above all cloud or colour one's view of reality, of what happens around one. The truth is brought home to us, of which we read concerning the great ones of tragedy, that human pride is at the root of error.

The closed mind is not shut by virtue but by selfishness. To live with human sympathy, with an embracing power of interest and of realization, your " broad-minded " man cannot but be partly a good man. One who sincerely recites the " Homo sum . . . nil alienum " must have had some personal acquaintance with the strength of human nature not merely with its weaknesses.

Sanctity is needed for balance and truth of outlook. All knowledge would naturally lead to action, and the acts of a man tend to affect his knowledge. We are one piece.

WHY POETRY FOR THE PIOUS ?

A pious soul might ask : Why not action alone ? If sanctity be the aim of life, why read poetry instead of confining oneself to prayer and self-conquest ? Well, there is more than external connection between wisdom and goodness. Perfection is the fulness of suitable and proper being, is it not ? Certainly a Solomon can offend, but he was also capable, before becoming foolish, of greater knowledge, love and service. " For Wisdom is more active than all active things and reacheth everywhere by reason of her purity." The God-Man had perfect knowledge of God and creation from the vision of his Father. To know God, we must study with honest eye his creation and image. True, a holy man might come to us and say : " I have neither leisure nor favourable circumstances in which to achieve the fulness of manhood explicitly ; I have only time for the most part of my day to try for it implicitly in one virtue, say, zeal or mortification, and I think that God will, on account of my absorption in this, supply my deficiencies." We could answer : " It is time for you to leave school, but the fuller ideal remains."

STUDY OBJECTIVE

I do not mean to imply that we should study literature with one eye open to our self-improvement. No. Study should be objective. For what is study but a zealous attempt to find out what things are, without and within us ? Self-examination without an outer norm, even this self-examination is self centred. Concentration upon the way we are doing something leads to defeat in the moves of chess or war. In educating ourselves, let us seek an object rather than to improve ourselves. This objectivity calls for patient energy. It is childlike and yet, paradoxically, the quality we associate with the father of the family. This objectivity Chesterton in "The Ballad of the White Horse" selects as Alfred's victorious quality, "He was least distant from the child piling the stones all day." Objectivity will prevent fadism and all the ills of egoism. It is the root in soil that is watered. An author, revealing either himself or others, is in danger of playing the cad unless he has the honesty of an Augustine which gives the right to self-expression. This honesty or humility denotes here that gaze which looks at truth apart from our desire and at self as if at a thing apart. We want the "single eye." Poetry does not invent new wonder. It needs no new mystery nor light such as never was on land or sea. It is wonderful if earth and common things, the truth, the real, are wonderful.

THERE HAS BEEN WRONG; NOTHING'S YET CLEARLY SEEN

The world is under our nose. Something seems not quite right in the tired dust that rests on nature's leaves and streams, in the gasses of a closed room, in the worn, ignoble monotony of the human heart. It is what makes the art of words so often seem froth. As Stephen Spender puts it for every one of us:

"What I had not foreseen
Was the gradual day."—

Successive sameness lacks the unity necessary to an artist's piece of work. As variety in structure is necessary for the living things we know that move as units, so it is necessary for poetry which imitates such life.

A WORD FOR THINGS

But not all the dust in the world can cover the plain evidence for wonder. This book as a whole is meant to state that it is in the plain facts, the humdrum, that mystery and wonder lurk, the seeds of poetry and literature. Such a petty thing as our humankind can be the cause of awe and diffidence. Wonder is in these things around us. And poetry is a word for things.